Blood-Lust Chickens and Renegade Sheep: A First Timer's Guide to Country Living

by Nick and Anita Evangelista

D1378809

Loompanics Unlimited
Port Townsend, Washington

Blood-Lust Chickens and Renegade Sheep: A First
  Timer's Guide to Country Living
© 1999 by Nick and Anita Evangelista

Published by:
Loompanics Unlimited
PO Box 1197
Port Townsend, WA 98368

Loompanics Unlimited is a division of Loompanics Enterprises, Inc.
1-360-385-2230
e-mail: service@loompanics.com
Web site: www.loompanics.com

Cover art and interior illustrations by Shary Flenniken
Photographs by Nick and Anita Evangelista

ISBN 1-55950-197-9
Library of Congress Card Catalog 99-65458

ɞ

Contents

൬

ଓଃ

This book is dedicated
To the memory of
J.L. Kimbrough

ଓଃ

୬

Acknowledgements

To the wise ones who have been our teachers: Russ BigDog, Uncle Deedah, Hardliner, Ct Vronsky, Dave, Will Continue, Diane Squire, Steve Heller, Outings R Us, Gordon, Old Git, Andy, Leo Champion, de, Invar, King of Spain, Jon Williamson, Nabi Davidson, Robert Cooke, Ashton and Leska in Cascadia, Lane Core, Jr., Ed Yourdon, Ed Yardeni, Gary North, Scott Olmsted, Rick Cowles, Cory Hamasaki and the saintly Robert Waldrop.

And to those who have taught us the folly of false pride and self-deception: Stephen Poole, Paul Davis, Y2KPro, cpr, Doc Paulie, Troll Maria, Hoffmeister, Jimmy Bagga Doughnuts, Mr. Decker, Norm.

May we find the New Millenium opens and continues with abundant light, warmth, and prosperity...

— Nick and Anita Evangelista

୬

C

✍

"Security is mostly a superstition. It does not exist in nature, nor do the children of men as a whole experience it. Avoiding danger is no safer in the long run than outright exposure. Life is either a daring adventure or nothing."— **Helen Keller**

✍

About This Book

Our goal in writing a book about the hazards of farm and country was not to be disparaging of the experience. We had, and have, no intention of scaring off potential homesteaders with horrors of blood-lusting chickens and renegade sheep. The whole truth of the matter is that living in rural America, or rural anywhere, can be a tough, godawful proposition.

We love living in the country and we enjoy our farm. Each day is a picture framed in gold, an adventure rich with feeling and experience. We would no more think of moving back to the city than we would of living at the bottom of the sea. But it's taken us a good many years to get the swing of farm life. I mean, really get it. Yet, we've known other folks, too many of them, who folded early in the game, people who had a genuine desire for a new life, but who gave up when they encountered that last straw. They hadn't been ready for real country living.

What they thought they'd get was that endless, clean, warm spring day. When fantasy collided with the less than perfect, cold hard facts of the farm, they simply self-destructed.

It would be great if everyone moving to a rural setting succeeded, but that is not the case. Even established farmers, who know what's what, fail.

This, then, is a book about real country experiences, failures and successes. It is also about the thoughts and attitudes that can make or break a life in the country.

Remember, thoughts create reality.

— Nick and Anita Evangelista

☾☽

ೞ

Introduction

This book might have been called *Fourteen Years of Living Heck in the Ozark Mountains or Mugged By Sheep*. The implication is that living in the country isn't necessarily a fun thing. It can be. But there are a lot of variables that can intrude into your life. An unexpected bit of violent weather that floods a nearby river leaves you cut off from the world. A neighbor's escaped bull runs you up a tree. A raccoon decides your chicken coop is his own private cafeteria. The list of possibilities is endless. There are times when you get up in the morning, and you think you know pretty well what you're going to be doing, but by the end of the day nothing you did even slightly resembles those early thoughts.

You just never know.

When we moved from Los Angeles to our farm in the Missouri Ozark Mountains in 1985, we thought we pretty much knew it all. We'd read all the best books and subscribed to all the best magazines. We were ready for anything the country had to throw at us, we thought. We told our friends back in Los Angeles that living in the country would be just like living in the city, only with fewer people around. Well, that proved to be wrong the very first day when a big black snake decided to be the first entity in the neighborhood to welcome us to the farm. Talk about shocks. We'd never even seen a snake outside the zoo before. And that was only the start. It got worse. If we'd had the money to move back to safe and sane Los Angeles right then, we just might have done that.

A big black snake welcomed us to the farm.
We'd never seen a snake outside the zoo before.

Things got better, of course, and they got a lot worse. Which is doubtlessly true of all things in life. But the point of this is that in the country, when you are expecting absolute paradise, and you get something else, it can knock you for a loop.

It's a fact that even people who've lived their entire lives in the country can burn out on a steady diet of things rustic. So, imagine coming to a farm cold turkey from a life, say, maybe thirty minutes from downtown Los Angeles. And we did it without safety helmets.

We weren't ready for the country; we should have known better. All days would be warm. All animals would be almost human. All ideas would succeed. All hardships would vanish. Nothing bad happens in the Promised Land.

We have known countless people over the years who've moved to the country, and who've moved away from the country. In fact, we tried to sell our farm twice a number of years ago, but had the deals go awry. We finally decided that Someone was trying to tell us something, and we gave up that idea.

Come hell or high water, the farm is our home.

But what about all those others, the ones who managed to sell their farms, or just walked away from them, leaving the remains for the bank to pick over? Well, they weren't so lucky, were they?

And, yet, there'll be someone reading this right now who'll be saying, "That could never happen to me. I know better. I have money. I have tools. I have books. What else do I need? I will soar above all problems. I will survive. I will thrive." We just remind ourselves that even millionaires kill themselves. Having stuff doesn't save you. You need that extra bit in your brain to pull you through.

That extra bit is what this book is about.

The End of the World, Y2K, Space Aliens, the Country, and You

A friend whose hobby is finding proof of the imminent collapse of human existence, believes when such an event occurs she will be beamed up into the safety of outer space by UFO aliens. She recently mailed us a clipping from a Los Angeles-based magazine dealing with the impaired quality of life existing in that city. Sort of a "My god, it's all true!" gesture on her part. She's also started, of late, sending us all sorts of Y2K info, which ranges from Mad Max end-of-the-world-as-we-know-it scenarios, to get-ready-just-in-case suggestions.

There are a lot of proposed reasons these days for escaping from the Big City, from "ain't the country neat" to millennialist blues.

When we hear people expounding on escaping the city, we usually shake our heads. Not because we think leaving the city is necessarily a bad idea — we did it ourselves — it's the matter-of-fact quality of these recommendations that bother us considerably. Like you can move to the country, and it'll be easy. Just go, and leave all your problems behind you. This advice is offered to people who've never been on a dirt road or raised anything bigger than a dog.

We've read even more adamant stuff on Internet pages where people are actually falling for this escape plan in droves. You know something? It's hard enough getting used to living in the country in the best of times. If someone thinks they're going to accomplish it in a total societal breakdown, they are nuts. They will have neither the knowledge nor the psychological wherewithal to cope. If things get as bad as they believe, and strangely, in some cases, hope for, they will die.

Certainly, there is a city arrogance in this type of thinking. How bad can living in the country be?

Pretty bad.

Pretty good, too. But the bad can do you in fast, like a sharp blow to the head.

So how do you survive a move back-to-the-land in any kind of situation? It is, we think, the people with a high tolerance for boredom, disaster, and simplicity who survive. Also, those who have an ability to improvise and roll with the punches. Where does this ability come from? It doesn't come from having stuff. We think it comes from having a mindset geared toward enduring and surviving. A realistic idea for what one might encounter in any situation is a must. Fantasy doesn't make it in the country.

Many country-oriented books or magazines ignore the less-than-ideal features about rural life, the same way a chamber of commerce ignores the fact that its city or town has crime and slums. It's bad for business to talk about those things. They just don't exist. But what do you do when you find yourself smack dab in the middle of the ignored negative reality? Basically, you sink.

You need reality from the start.

ଔ

ଔ

Chapter One
To Move or Not to Move?

When you move to the country, your life becomes your own.
Within the realm of civilized thought and common sense,
you can do pretty much as you please.

Benefits

Most people who move to the country aren't motivated by riches and fame. Anyone who equates such a move with wealth and power will be, more often than not, quickly disabused of the notion. The few exceptions usually start their venture with a good deal of money. This, then, does not relate to most of us.

Once situated in the country, you have to remind yourself regularly that there really are benefits to living in the country. The difficult parts of your new life can be very distracting. When you are kicked in the kneecap by your cow, or when you find that copperhead snake slithering across your kitchen floor, or when you discover what's left of your chickens after that unseen predator has finished with them, you don't say to yourself, "Oh, boy, do I ever love the country! This is so much better than living in ...(you name the city)." To the contrary, you will probably be questioning your very sanity for ever having wanted to move away from the city.

So, what exactly do you get, besides hard times, when you head off to the rurals? Well, first and foremost, there is freedom. FREEDOM! Your life becomes your own. Within the realm of civilized thought and common sense, you can do pretty much as you please. You are free of petty rules and regulations the city tacks on to the simplest of endeavors. If you want to build on to your house, you don't have to get yourself a thousand bureaucratically generated permits. All you need are the necessary materials and the skill. If you've got guts, you don't even need skill. If you do a good job, that's fine; if you do a lousy job, that's your responsibility. If you want to homeschool your children, that, too, is your business. You can raise the livestock that appeals to you. You want to populate your farm with a flock of emus, go for it. You can plant the plants you want. If you want your property to look awful, no one's going to report you to the plant police. Just stay way from growing recreational weeds. Those are illegal even in the country.

Mostly, though, your life is your own. Freedom is important. Freedom is a road map to the universe. Freedom and real life go together.

But, with all your new found freedom, you also develop a sense of responsibility, a feeling for the results of your actions. So, you don't mistreat your livestock, you don't burn your house down, you don't let your children terrorize the neighborhood with machetes. With responsibility, your life gains balance. Consequences come quickly in the country if you don't learn to direct yourself with self-discipline and intelligence. Freedom brings self-discipline or self-destruction.

Then there's the aspect of personal growth. By doing, you gain abilities you never thought you'd have. You become — and this one was important to us — competent. A problem solver, not a victim. Your car breaks down, you fix it; you don't just sit there and moan. You need to add a new electrical outlet to a wall in your house, you do it. You milk your goat, build a book shelf, deliver a lamb, repair a barbed wire fence line, and fix your tiller all in one day.

Of course, with all these new features in your life comes a sense of reality, a view of the world as it is, as opposed to the world that movies, television, and the news media force feeds you. Life suddenly slows down to a human pace so you see it, feel it, understand it. Reality is a useful commodity.

With a good look at reality, you also gain judgement. You can say this is good, and that is bad, and have reasons for your decisions. It is difficult to pull the wool over such a person's eyes. This can be useful when voting or buying a new car or watching the news on television.

Finally, at the bottom line, you claim your life, which you don't really own in the city, not really. When you claim your life, you return to the human race, and stop being a cog, a microchip, a thingamajig in the non-human entity called the civilized world, where people are numbers, food originates in supermarkets, feelings are limited by law to knee-jerk, feel-good reactions, and skills consist of button pushing and knowing which line to stand in.

Too, maybe you'd like to breathe some fresh air once in a while? They have that in the country, you know.

Surviving Your Move Back to the Land

Making it in the country is not a chance action, a flip of the coin. It takes a concerted effort, a plan, a change in the way you view the world. If you think you're going to take the day to day the same way you'd tackle your time in downtown New York City, you'll be doomed before you start your adventure.

You need to know what to do, but also what not to do. Which isn't as easy as it seems. There are so few right things to do, and so many wrong choices to make in the country. Of course, even with good choices, your new life can be a hard nut to crack. Think, then, how those bad decisions will affect you.

We don't include a lot of pat answers in this book. Each of our chapters are designed basically to get you to think, to start that inner dialogue, to get you to come up with your own solutions, the solutions that will fit your situation exactly. Rural Missouri is not rural Utah is not rural Connecticut is not rural Texas.

Take the thoughts we've presented, and run with them. Shape them to your life, and use them as guides and reminders. Being able to generate just one more idea, when you have no more ideas, is what keeps the flame alive. It's only when all hope is gone that you crumble.

Keep thinking.

When you move to the country, it is best if you are moving *to* something, instead of *away* from something. The result may seem the same: You are where you are. But, if you don't know the difference between the two, you will eventually find yourself in big trouble.

Moving *away* from something implies a backward looking thought process that dwells on the past, and lacks plans for the future. The important part, getting away, has been accomplished, so everything else is an anticlimax.

Moving *to* something implies a forward-looking point of view, a point of view with plans. There is hope and optimism, a can't-wait-to-get-there attitude. This is a world view of always becoming, hard work, and success.

Which attitude do you think would work best in the country?

Gauging Your Capacity

The book, *The Peter Principle*, dealt with people in business who are good at what they do up to a point, and then they are elevated to their level of incompetence, where they proceed to muck up not only their own affairs, but everyone else's.

You can do this on your farm to yourself.

When you begin any farm project, think small. If you're going to raise chickens or goats or ponies, start with a few, and work your way up. Then you can find out just what you can actually handle.

We raised sheep for many years. We had as many as seventy head at one time. We could raise sheep, but seventy was way too much for us, psychologically, which translated into too much physically. At this point, the flock suffered, we suffered, our fields suffered. It was just too much for us to focus on, even with our expertise. When we finally cut the flock down to between fifteen and twenty animals, we did just fine. We could handle that. That was our true psychological limit. We learned the hard way.

*It's best to think small in the beginning — start with
a few animals and work your way up.*

Some people can work with large numbers of animals. We've seen folks with two hundred rabbits. That's what they did. That was what they built their days around. And they were happy doing just that. We've known other people who couldn't keep one rabbit alive on a dare.

It's best to be honest about your capabilities up front. Know yourself from the start. Don't get cocky. Don't let your ego get in the way. If you're smart, you'll save yourself time and money and headaches.

You moved to the country for a better life, not a pain in the butt.

Your Expectations

You will have expectations about the area where you'll be moving to, about your possibilities, about the people. That's to be expected. Some things you'll encounter may be better than you could hope for, some things far worse. The best advice we can give you is this: Don't assume.

You won't know something for sure until you get to where you are going. Something may seem obvious to you, and yet, to the people you encounter in your new area, what you think may be totally unimportant.

C3

Nick: I thought, when I moved to the Ozarks, that I'd be a celebrity — because I was a fencing teacher who'd worked in film, because I'd had numerous articles published, because I'd worked with more than a few famous people.

I was wrong.

When I got to my new location, no one cared. No one was interested. Some people even thought it was funny. You'll be lucky if you ever get yourself one student, I was told more than once. People used to call me on the phone, and ask what kind of fences I built. They weren't joking. Some were actually put out that I wouldn't build fences for them, as though I was shirking my responsibility to the community. This was very discouraging, and a source of countless negative thoughts on my part. What was wrong with these people?

It took me a long time to understand that the area would never adapt to me, that I had to adapt my expectations and energies to fit the area. I just cooled my heels, and bided my time, and eventually the word got out to the people who would be interested in what I had to offer. It took two full years, though. Furthermore, realizing I'd never reach that many people interested in fencing if I simply continued to plug away at the local population, I changed my tack some, and started writing books. Because of that, I've been able to increase my teaching scope a thousandfold. Basically, I molded my own skills to fit the realities of the area.

Anita: *I did the same thing when I decided to take advantage of my interest in medical things, and went back to college to get my RN degree. No matter where you go, the world never runs out of sick people. So, I adapted, too.*

ଔ

So much in the country transpires, not through advertising, but through word-of-mouth. It's like water through coffee grounds: It takes time to percolate down, and turn into something you can use.

It's a fact that country people, small town people, too, are slow to accept change. That may seem very obstinate or stupid to big city folks who live in a speed-of-light changing environment. Actually, there is much stability and strength in that steadiness of thought, even if you don't like it. You can count on people to be what they are, and to say what they really think.

Don't expect anything else.

ଔ

C3

Chapter Two
Preparing to Move

Location, Location, Location

If you are used to other people being around,
then the population factor may be important to you.

Where you end up will be an important factor in whether
you succeed in your country move, or not. This not only has to

do with what part of the country you move to, but many other factors you may not have considered:

- How far you decide to live from a town
- Whether you live on a paved or dirt road
- What kind of neighbors you have
- The quality of the land you have purchased
- The type of predators you may be faced with
- Local water quality
- The proximity of prisons, nuclear reactors, or chemical dumps
- The severity of the average winters you'll be experiencing
- How deep your well is
- How your new home is situated with regard to rivers that might overflow, or dams that might break
- The economic outlook for your area
Furthermore:

If you are used to other people being around, then the population factor may be important to you. Is your nearest neighbor just down the road, or twenty miles away? Maybe you don't want anyone else right next to you. Or do you derive a sense of security from being near other families? Only you know the answer to these questions. Where we live, the population per square mile is 6.

Crime may be a factor, although it does tend to be less widespread where the cows outnumber the people. Still, in rural areas within, say, a 9- or 10-mile radius of growing towns, crime has a way of spilling out into the countryside — burglaries and vandalism, that kind of stuff.

Also, some people shy away from buying property too near national parks, which have a way of annexing new land, or simply restricting what neighbors do with their own property, because it's so close to government land.

Television reception may be an issue. Many rural areas have really crummy TV reception. This can come from being to far away from any television stations, or from living in a mountainous area where TV signals just can't get to you. If you are close enough to a town, cable is a possibility. Today, satellite dishes are available, too. But, if these are out of your scope, then you just might want to consider what you would do without TV.

How will any of these things affect you personally? Each person has his own tolerance level, his own coping abilities. A lot will ride on your motivations for moving to the country, and your specific expectations. Just the same, it's best to consider the circumstances surrounding your new home so you don't end up hitting a brick wall.

Our only for-sure advice: Stay away from active volcanoes. We think that's a good rule of thumb.

Dwellings

This may seem an odd thing to say, but live in a house, please! You might read in various sources how a family moved to the country and lived in a sod hut or a teepee or a cave. And that they loved it. Great! Don't try to follow in their footsteps. They were an exception to the rule. That's why they were written about. Most sane people don't go in for that kind of stuff. They doubtlessly had a high disgust threshold. Sod huts are great, if you don't mind sharing your home with worms!

Moving to the country will be stressful enough without having to get used to living in a junked school bus or an abandoned barn. Such possibilities may ring of economy, but they also scream doom! They are, by and large, possibilities only for the very young and adventurous or the seriously mentally impaired. One of us wanted to live in our 1972 Volkswagen bus when we began discussing a move to the country; luckily, the other one was able to talk her out of it. We know for certain we'd have attacked each other with ax handles in about a week if we'd gone through with that idea.

As for actual houses, watch out for the classic real estate agent come-on: "All this place needs is some work, and it'll be a showplace." This also means lots of money, time, energy, and patience. Lacking any one of the above may spell death for your country dream.

Watch out for the classic real estate agent come-on:
"All this place needs is some work, and it'll be a showplace."

We were fortunate to have an agent who was honest enough to give us the straight dope on the properties we looked at. "The only thing that'll fix this place up would be one stick of dynamite in the front door and one in the back door." He reminded us often that the only building code in the country is "don't build on your neighbor's property." We can recall looking at a farmhouse where the owners had knocked out the downstairs supporting wall to make their living room bigger, and when the upstairs started to sag downward, they simply shored it up with unreinforced 2-by-4s. That was a house just waiting to become a pile of lumber. We did not consider it. Also, indoor plumbing and electricity will be an issue for you, even if you don't think so initially. These things only seem small until you don't have them.

Watch out for dry rot. Dry rot looks nice when it's been painted, but it doesn't do much to enhance the quality or the value of your house. Fixing big cracks in foundations can eat up a savings account. Beware of houses built near river banks or on obvious flood plains. Brand new outdoor siding might be hiding some unusual structural horrors. And watch out for houses that have changed hands frequently in a short period of time; maybe you don't want to find out why. And what's that big stain on the carpet? Could be blood.

Keep all these things in mind when you decide on that country home, and you just might find something you'll really like the day after you move into it.

Moving

You might not think it, but even if you really enjoy the thought of moving to the country, moving itself is going to be stressful. There's no way around it. Moving from one city to another city is stressful. Moving from a city to a rural setting is doubly stressful. For the city mind, there is little or nothing familiar in this new experience to grasp to steady the psyche. Then you start forgetting about why you moved in the first place. No matter how strong your motivation was to move, you forget. The move can drive some people nuts. There were moments during our move, and right after it, that we came pretty close to hitting the brick wall. We got extremely thin-skinned for a while, and it didn't take much to get a good rumble going. We'd walk around grumbling like Fred C. Dobbs in *Treasure of the Sierra Madre*. Someone would say, "What a nice day!" And someone else would say, "So you're telling me how to think now!" And the fight would be on.

We eventually remembered why we moved to the country, and calmed down.

Moving is stressful. Don't let it do you in before you even get started.

❦

ᔅ

Chapter Three
You're There. Now What?

Reality Descends Hard

You rarely read about real hardship or serious life problems
in your average back-to-the-land literature. When fact and fancy
fail to mesh, and reality descends with a resounding,
painful thud, it is often too much to take.

The good news is that you're finally living on your own farm in the country. You've scrimped and saved, and now your dream has come true...

The bad news is: (a.) A 6-foot blacksnake has taken up residence in your living room wall. (b.) Little Bobby has just come in from the woods covered from head to foot in seed ticks, maybe a zillion of them. (c.) The chickens have just eaten your entire tomato crop. (d.) The goat has just developed a new skill — kicking over the milk bucket, but only when it's full. (e.) The rabbits refuse to breed. (f.) A former furry creature of the wild is presently decomposing in an inaccessible corner under your kitchen floor. (g.) Your car, unused to the arbitrary harshness of dirt roads, now sounds like a gas-combustion maraca. (h.) The cow died. (i.) Your dog Fluffy has run off after a raccoon, and is now officially missing in action. (j.) Everything has stomach worms.

Worse yet, this is better than what it was last week.

Suddenly, that back-to-the-land dream is looking more like the plot of a novel co-authored by James Herriot and Stephen King. And suddenly you're whispering to yourself, "What the heck alternate dimension have I fallen into? This ain't what I expected. I can't take it. I want out. Ahhhhhhhhhhhhhhhg!"

When sanity returns, you're flipping burgers in Simi Valley, and you sort of recall that you once personally knew a chicken by its first name.

Bye, bye, rural America.

So, what the heck went wrong?

The answer is, you found out the hard way — and way too late — that living in the country is not one long spring day. There are adversities by the score, and more than a little hard work goes into every little bit of progress you make. Many folks are ignorant of this — or just plain disregard it, thinking that they know better — when they say goodbye to the big city and head off for a new life in the country. You rarely read about real hardship or serious life problems in your average back-to-the-land literature. We've never seen a story titled, *My Farm and My Divorce,* or *Three Years on the Farm and Six Months in the Stress Ward.*

So, when fact and fancy fail to mesh, and reality descends with a resounding, painful thud, it is often too much to take. It is a sad truth, but many people do give up totally, and go trudging back to the urban jungle. Maybe if they'd started out with a more balanced view of farm stuff, they would have first developed the mental resources to survive.

When we moved, we had feelings of hope and promise brimming inside us. Living in the country would be wonderfully easy, we thought. Then, we found out the truth. Immediately. The country wastes no time on know-nothing beginners.

Obviously, living in the country can be a rewarding, stimulating, and highly pleasant existence (and it has been all these things for us); but the rurals also have a darker side, a psychologically dangerous side that can't be overlooked, or underplayed, if one plans to succeed in one's back-to-the-land quest.

Self-Sufficiency

Self-sufficiency must almost be like a religion in the country. If you've lived in the city for most of your life, you will have to cultivate this ability. Not necessarily in the sense of knowing everything and having all kinds of tools and objects and guns and hidden caches of food at your disposal. We're talking about an attitude, a readiness to jump in and do, improvising or making do if you have to. Realizing that out in the boonies, away from the reassuring assistance of the all-knowing experts — repairmen or whatever — you will have to deal with crisises and problems on your own, that you will have to count on your own resolve and mental stamina to keep from being beaten down by adversity. The ability to simply endure is often the making or breaking of a back-to-the-land person.

Eventually, you may end up having to be your own vet, electrician, plumber, carpenter, painter, or VCR-repair person. You have to be ready to take on these things — at least mentally — so when difficult situations arise, they don't leave you in the corner staring at dust bunnies.

ᙍ

An Example

Nick: When our bathroom water pipes shattered after an extremely cruel and lengthy January freeze during our first winter in the Ozarks, I didn't know what we were going to do. At the time, we weren't in a position financially to call a plumber out to our farm. A sense of doom swept over us. Our water system was unusable. I'd never thought about plumbing before — it was something guys with pipes and wrenches and sagging, baggy pants did. I'd never even been under our house before. We didn't even know where to turn off the water main. Everything was new. What could we do?

Well, the sound of Niagara Falls roaring under our bathroom floor was an excellent motivator. We quickly figured out how to cut off the water flow. Then, feeling a bit more in control of the situation, Anita and I sat down and figured out the how-to, how-much, and where-to-get questions. Having no water for the rest of our lives was not a viable alternative. After a few phone calls to local hardware stores, we knew just

*what had to be done, and what it would cost. We could afford
to fix the damage — if we did the labor ourselves.*

*To be honest, the fixing end of the project was not fun. Nor
was it all that easy. There was the discomfort of lying on my
back, beneath the house, in a pool of freezing mud. My
muscles cramped and my fingers ached. But I survived. I
ended up having to redo my repair job twice, until I managed
to perfect the art of connecting pipes so they wouldn't leak. In
the end, though, we had a water system we could count on.*

*(By the way, subsequent broken pipes during other winters
have been, more or less, a piece of cake.)*

∞

Another Opportunity

Your opportunities for self-sufficiency may be based
somewhat on your finances. But we'd suggest you grab those
moments and run with them. New skills won't hurt you. And
once you have them, they'll be there for all emergencies.

Basic car repair is a big deal, especially on country roads.
With all respect to John Denver, country roads won't take you
home, or to town, if your car is dead on a back road. The
ability to change tires is a must, as is a fundamental
understanding of how your car engine works. We've had to
replace the fuel pump, the carburetor, the distributor, the
thermostat, the alternator, and the master cylinder on an
automotive dinosaur, starting with zero knowledge. But when
you think about the part costing $15 and the labor costing
$100, that can be a pretty good incentive. You may have to
fiddle with things for a bit. But learning is not impossible.
Nick began his car repair education at the age of 37.

Close Encounters

Butchering your own livestock is something else you might find yourself having to do. It is not fun. And, hopefully, it never will be. But, if you need meat, and you can't afford to take the animal to a processing plant, you do it yourself. Or you become a vegetarian.

We have butchered sheep, goats, rabbits, chickens, ducks, quail, and turkeys; and we have yet to turn into chainsaw-murdering maniacs. Butchering becomes a natural process, in which you take pride for being efficient and humane. You're taking on a big responsibility, interacting intimately with life and death, and you know where your food comes from. Which many city folks simply will never grasp. That's a bit of reality that's as old as humankind.

Other Possibilities

You might also have to tackle carpentry and masonry, fence building, cutting and splitting fire wood, and hunting. Who knows, maybe one day you'll have to save the earth from invading space aliens.

You have to learn all kinds of stuff.

Be ready.

You have to at least be ready.

Tools

Back-to-the-land types, fortunately, have a lot of confidence in their ability to adapt to their new situation. Along with confidence, however, you will need appropriate tools. Just as you wouldn't try to repair a VCR with a hammer (at least, not if you expected it to work when you were done!), you also wouldn't expect to do the various work your homestead will need without correct equipment.

Here are the basics we've found critically important:

- Hammers (three different sizes and weights), with nails of all types and lengths.
- Staple gun, long and short staples.
- Wrenches of all sizes, screwdrivers (Phillips and flathead), pliers, wire cutters, heavy scissors, ratchet sets. ...and, we guarantee, no matter how complete the set, you will one day find a screw or nut that none of your tools will fit...
- Duct tape and WD-40. Million-and-one-uses.
- Garden hoes — the "real" kind, not the clunky junk they sell at hardware stores. "Real" hoes, generally made prior to the 1960s, are lightweight, carefully sharpened, and are surprisingly well-balanced. After you've used one of these babies, you'll spurn the modern stuff forever. Check for real hoes at garage and farm sales — that's where we found ours.
- Garden hoses, ½-inch heavy-duty ones. They cost $15-20 each, way more than the $5 ones, but they can tolerate a lot more abuse — you can drive over them for years and leave 'em out in the sun, and they hold up to it.
- Garden cart. Sold by various names and in various styles, this is the one truly indispensable garden implement. You can really transport goods in these — 400 pounds of dirt or manure, 3 to 5 bales of hay at a time, or a passel of squealing kiddies out for a ride. Because of the way they are balanced, you don't have to strain your back to lift as you would with a wheel barrow.
- Flat and pointed shovels, pickax, post hole digger. How else are you going to get that 400 pounds of dirt into your garden cart? Or plant your orchard?
- Fence post pounder, fence wire stretcher. You won't need this unless you are putting in metal fence posts — but then, you've gotta have it.

- Saws — manual, electric and gasoline-powered. Hacksaws. Good sturdy crosscut saws will have more uses than you realize. When your arm poops out, you can switch to your $50 circular saw for a while. If you will be harvesting your own firewood, you'll probably want a chain saw: Get a good one. Don't skimp. The better brands will last for years, saw cleanly and accurately, and have safety features that will help prevent sawing your ears off. The cheap models will give you nothing but grief. This tool will keep you warm in the winter — so it might as well be one that is easy and joyful to work with.
- Maul, ax, wedges. For making your wood small enough to fit in the stove.
- Gloves. Leather for work, heavy wool for winter. Be sure to use a good oil (such as olive oil) on your hands in the winter to prevent dryness and those awful cracks.
- Plumbing supplies, including extra lengths of pipes, joints, caps, sealing compound, glue, valves, and replacement faucets. Your pipes will break in winter, when the plumber can't possibly get to you — you'll need to be able to patch the system (or repair it!) on your own. These supplies will let you get your water running again!
- Plastic 5-gallon buckets. These are another of the "indispensable" items for which there are a million uses. You can buy these (at exorbitant prices), or acquire them from bakeries (frosting mix comes in them), from fast food restaurants (dill pickle slices), or from delis (more pickles). Just ask.
- GOOD spare tires. Well, okay, they're not really tools. But you will get a flat when your spares are all flat otherwise. And you might throw a few canisters of that "flat fixer" stuff into the trunk, just in case.

- Air canister. This will be useful when you need to air-up the flat spare but can't find the "flat fixer" goo — and a nice good-neighbor gesture when your neighbor's spare is flat, too.
- Generator, if you must. Good when the power goes off and you have to pump up water (make sure it is SURGE-rated so that it will start your pump), or keep the freezer on for a brief period of time. Don't plan on using a generator as your only permanent power source, unless you're really into spending large sums of money and getting very little in return.
- "Strike anywhere" matches, candles, oil lamps (Aladdin brand has superior light), extra mantles and wicks, and plenty of oil. The power will go off; you will be glad you have these.
- CB radio or long-range walkie-talkie. Send one with the kids when they go out for a hike — you won't worry as much. You can take one out to the field when you are checking on the critters. You can even carry them while in the mall so that everybody can be located! Plus, they're really fun.
- Boots/cross-trainers. In the summer when weather is good, a comfortable pair of cross-trainers is the most useful shoe you can have. Yes, yes, yes, we know "cowboys" wear pointy mid-calf boots in the summer ...have you ever seen the condition of their toes and toenails???? It's a horror, the stress those feet are put through. Sharply pointed shoes of any kind will ruin your precious tootsies, and give you foot trouble for the rest of your life — it isn't worth it to look fashionable. For winter, a good pair of wool-lined "waders" with a strong leather upper will give you years of warm and comfy use. Be sure to oil the leather when you take them out of storage, and again when you put them back.

- Tiller. We've had many brands ...and been happiest with our little 5-hp Troy-bilt. You can garden without a tiller (and we did, for about 12 years), but a good tiller makes the whole process that much easier and more productive.
- Lawnmower or lawntractor. Yes, we have used sheep to mow our lawn... they do a pretty good job, and add free fertilizer, too! But if you're mowing an area where sheep and goats would be a problem (an orchard, for example), the answer is a mechanical mower. You can find push-type mowers around still (though it will kill you to use one if your grass is much more than 6 inches high), electric mowers (run for 3 to 4 hours per charge), and gas-powered ones. The last category has all types of variations, from the $100 cheapie which will probably only last one season — to the $3,600 mower/tractor, with multiple uses. If you're mowing more than an acre, the lawn tractor is probably the best idea, and you can find them in the $800-$1,200 range. Some varieties can also be found that include tillers and cart-pullers, so these can be an all-purpose tool on the farm. (Just make sure you have backups, for the day the lawn tractor won't start!)
- Ice cleats to slip over your boots. You'll only need them for a brief period during the winter, but you'll be eternally grateful. Believe us.
- A .22 rifle. At least. Many new BTLers think they can carry on without any weapons. We did. We dispatched our chickens with an ax, sheep and goats with a heavy stick and knife, and pigs by hauling them off to the butcher shop...where the butcher used a .22. If we had to "put down" a horse or a cow, the ONLY way is with a rifle. Ever try to discourage a marauding raccoon, high in the rafters of your barn with a chicken in its grasp — with a stick??? Ever seen a raccoon laugh??? How about a coyote, running across

your field with a bawling lamb clasped in its jaws? Your animals depend on you for their food, water, and protection — we may not like it, but we have to do it.

- Pickup truck or other transportation vehicle. For many years, we drove a '67 Chevy Suburban — a totally decrepit, worn out truck that smoked continuously and sometimes decided it didn't have to stop when the brakes were put on. But it hauled tons upon tons of hay, brought animals home and took them away, and did nearly all the important heavy-hauling chores we had to do. And generally cost less than $50 per year for repairs and parts (we did a lot of the work ourselves). A good truck is a working partner... save the 4-cylinder economy car for trips to the mall.

Everything in its Time (Backups for the Backups)

You're prepared for the big move... you've figured out what you want, where you wish to go, and have a pretty good idea of how you'd like to live. You probably already have an internal image of yourself at your new place, puttering, or gardening, or surveying the glorious outcome of your labors. These are good things.

But, perhaps at the same time, your real-world residence looks like a cross between Oliver and Lisa's *Green Acres* and something from *Tobacco Road*. It isn't the way you want it to be... yet.

There is SO much to do!

What's first? Then what?

An Order Checklist

Permit us to offer a guideline for where to start and go next — you get the benefit of our mistakes!

The First Year

1. The house: Make it livable, not the neighborhood envy. Patch the roof so it doesn't rain indoors. Put up screens to keep the flies and mosquitoes out. Lay traps for the mice and rats. Replace bad plumbing. Clean and inspect the chimney. Caulk around door frames and windows. Replace broken glass. Put up storm windows. Depending on the house, this could be a full month's work. Save the major renovations (insulating, replacing old windows, painting, updating all the appliances) for next year. Somewhere in the middle of this turmoil, bake some cookies. Visit the neighbors. Visit local churches. It'll give you something to talk about while you're caulking.

2. Walk and check all fence lines. Make some notes on the spots that need to be repaired or replaced. Order supplies.

3. Till garden area. Plan garden, order or buy seeds locally (2 days). Plant in garden if late spring, or begin indoors in flats if early spring (2 days).

4. Decide which livestock you are ready to own (cows might be too big for your current needs, for example; horses might be nothing more than an interesting diversion, better for later, and so forth). Begin with only one (1!) species if you have not raised livestock before — and chickens or rabbits are a good place to start. All livestock need shelter and fences. Determine if your current facilities are adequate, or whether they need improvement.

5. Investigate livestock you will acquire — call local people and order chicks. Know the date that you must have your facility ready to accept the critters.

6. Complete your fences, fix the livestock shelters.

7. Repair ponds, or prepare watering systems for the barns and shelters.

8. Order and stock appropriate livestock grain, and include appropriate amount of good quality hay.

9. Accept delivery of livestock species #1. Makes changes and adjustments in your facility, as needed.

Birds such as chickens, turkeys, and ducks are popular with back-to-the-land types. It's a good idea to begin with only one species if you have not raised livestock before — chickens are a good place to start.

10. Settle in for a while. You've got a garden to tend, and livestock to take care of a couple times a day. You've discovered some local predators like your livestock as much as you do. You've found that money doesn't go as far as it used to — but you can make it stretch even further. Make time to really get to know your neighbors.

11. Begin preparations for winter. Determine your wood or fuel needs. Send some extra money to the electric company, if you're on the line (so you can pay a little less later).

12. Cut, haul, and stack wood. Check the outside of the house for winter-readiness. Patch or fill cracks, pull bird's nests out of eaves. Watch out for wasps and hornets!

13. Can and preserve garden, as needed. Decide if you will need a fruit cellar next year. When garden is exhausted, retill, fertilize, and put it to bed.

14. Make some Christmas gifts from scratch... they cost less and people love 'em. Make certain livestock shelter will protect them from cold winds and severe weather.

15. Stack some firewood on the porch. Make a bet on the first day of snow. Check the fireplace or wood stove for leaky gaskets, and ensure a good attachment to the chimney. Put in fire extinguishers (even a box of baking soda will do in a pinch) and smoke alarms.

16. Assume you will be iced in for part of the winter, and stock up on amusements (such as games, cards, and cassette recorders), extra batteries, flashlights, and so forth. Assume you will not be able to acquire feed for the livestock for a month — and stock up appropriately.

17. Survive winter. Make notes on what needs to be improved for next year.

Year Two

1. List all the things you wished you had last winter, start acquiring now.

2. Begin seeds for garden indoors in February and March. Order or buy seeds and plan garden. Include extras if you found you ran out of some particular item.

3. Review livestock survival. Change shelter and adjust feeding to improve the odds for next year. Decide if you need another animal — goats are a good #2, if you've never raised livestock.

Goats are a good second species for the novice farmer.

4. First good day in spring, till garden. Plant peas, lettuce, bok choy, other frost-hardy items, and protect with extra hay.

5. Walk fence lines, and make notes on where repairs are needed. Warm days in spring are good times to paint outdoors.

6. Decide where a good spot for the home-orchard would be... maybe this year? Maybe next?

7. When the grass is up, turn livestock out to fields for only a few hours daily to accustom them to the lush growth.

Deworm, dust for lice, vaccinate animals as needed. If there are new babies, make sure they get their first shots and are suckling or eating well before letting them follow mothers to fields.

8. Contact your hay supplier and compliment him or her on the quality — let 'em know you'll want some more this year, if available. Agree on price, if possible (some changes may occur if the weather doesn't cooperate).

9. Decide what improvements *must* be made on the house. Clean and repair chimneys, notice how much extra wood is left over (or how much extra you had to acquire!). Plan to have two times the amount of wood you'll need for next winter.... just in case.

10. Stock up! See #8 through #17 in Year One.

Years Three through Five

Add livestock species #3, 4, and 5. Make sure you include a livestock guardian dog and a rat terrier-type dog. Keep a barn cat. Make sure all animals have up-to-date vaccinations (rabies is especially important). Check fences once per year and repair or replace. Plan and plant orchard area. Expand the garden. Improve the house — add an extra bathroom, if possible. Increase the size of the pantry, put in a root cellar if wanted. Make backup systems for your backup systems. Throw out or recycle or give to thrift shops all the junk you kept from your old life that doesn't work in your new life. Make time for some community or church-supporting activities.

Backups for the Backups

With a little time under your belt, you can see that even the best-laid plans have a way of going awry. This is why it is prudent to have a backup for every major system you require — and a backup for the backup.

For instance, we get our water from a well — it is pumped up by an electric pump. As backups, we might have: a generator to run the pump if the power fails; some well-buckets (they fit directly down the well casing) to pull up water if the power fails AND the generator fails; some stored bottled water, if we can't use the well-buckets; a cistern, if there is no power whatsoever; plus a nearby pond and a river within a quarter mile. Now, clearly, we didn't actually plan all of these backups... but, we know we have a water source, no matter what happens.

In the same way, having a backup food source is important — suppose this year's garden fails? It's a long wait until spring! A supply of home-canned food, some supermarket canned goods, a big and filled freezer, a root cellar, even cans of freeze-dried/dehydrated emergency foods are all REASON-ABLE and PRUDENT. You just don't know what will happen in the future — from job layoffs to illness to civil strife. Just be sure to rotate your stock so that there are always fresh goods on hand.

Backup heat? For many years we heated only with wood. It's a lot of work, especially for the old folks we're turning into! Last year, we heated for the first time with propane ...it cost a lot more, but saved wear and tear on our backs! Even so, our kitchen stove is STILL a wood-fired cooker, and we STILL keep a year's supply of firewood stacked in the yard. If the propane guys can't reach us for any reason, we'd still be warm and toasty. And if, heaven forbid, we should run out of firewood, we can close off most of the house, and we've got heavy down-filled garments, plenty of sweaters, thick socks, and woolen hats to keep us warm.

Now, suppose (heaven forbid) our house should become unlivable through fire or natural disaster — what then? We've still got a barn, root cellar, and a roomy Chevy van as backups

— and even know where a pretty nice cave is located! It isn't exactly like home, but it's better than sitting in the rain!

Water. Food. Heat. Shelter. These are the crucial elements for which you must have backups — you can live quite comfortably if the VCR poops out on you, or if the washer breaks down, but if the Big Four of Survival aren't there, well then, neither are you.

Make your plans!

Stocking Up: A Hind-Sight Perspective

So, just how crummy can things get out on a farm?

Here's a sampling from one winter we had about ten years ago. I wrote all this down as it happened, so it's pretty much accurate, including the groans, screams, and oofs.

Here goes:

It began simply enough with rain. Lots and lots and lots of rain. It came down in buckets. Buckets the size of brontosaurs. And, suddenly, the regular road leading out of our valley, the road that passed with a normally innocent dip through a river bed, was impassible. Impassible beneath 5 feet of muddy, rushing, quarrelsome water. Tree trunks the size of trucks sped downstream. This was an imposition, but it was hardly lethal. Anita and I had to go to town, so we detoured on a lesser used back road to get to the main highway, one that didn't go anywhere near the river.

We made it to town. We shopped. Then, we drove homeward along that same route we'd traveled earlier. It was an overcast night. No moon, no stars. It was dark, the way only a deserted country road, a road with no street lights, can be dark. A lonely, consuming blackness, like the inside of empty. So, we never saw the tree branch stretched across the rutted road before we hit it. Too late — we felt a slight bump and heard a raspy, dragging sound. My wife stopped the car. I got out, and dislodged the wood. At the same moment, Anita noticed the brake light go on, blinking red, on the dashboard. When she tried the brakes, they were gone. We drove home slowly, in first gear, a lack of speed and momentum our only stopping device.

When we rolled to a feeble stop in front of our farm, I jumped out of the car, and checked for damage under the car with a flashlight. The brake line on the right rear wheel, where the offending branch had embedded itself, was broken. Brake fluid dripped in a steady stream from the wound.

We now had a car that would not stop voluntarily. That's a no-no even in rural America. We could no longer drive. We were stranded.

This was just before Christmas.

Of course.

Soon after this, I came down with some sort of skin rash. I'm not sure what it was. It just itched like crazy. A neighbor had offered me free hay, if I'd only clean it out of his barn. His cattle had tromped some of it down, but most of it was still ok. He wanted it out so he could put some horse stalls in the barn. I jumped at the chance for free hay. For our sheep.

I did the job.

That night, I broke out in awful, itchy blotches. There must have been something in the hay that didn't agree with me. The irritation first appeared on my neck, then spread quickly to other parts. The itch was the kind that makes scratching your skin off with a screwdriver seem reasonable, even fun. In a few days, my neck was a solid expanse of raw red. I looked like I had the worst case of sunburn since they invented skin.

In desperation, I turned to home remedies. Since we were trapped at home, I didn't have much of a choice. I rubbed caster oil on the rash. It didn't help. I tried cod liver oil. I think that helped to make my skin feel a little better, but it didn't do much for the way I smelled. I smelled like a stinking fish boat. I once woke up one night with a cat sitting on my chest, greedily licking my neck. I wondered absently when it was going to start eating, and went back to sleep.

Anita kept saying, "Oh, stop scratching. It'll go away in a few days." It didn't.

Next came the freezing weather. Snow fell. Three or four inches. We were going to have our first white Christmas on our farm. A neighbor promised to fix our car's brakes, but he couldn't as long as there was snow on the ground. More days without transportation.

We were going to have our first white Christmas on the farm.
Christmas came and went, very quietly.

The snow finally departed a week later when the temperature shot up abruptly to 55 degrees. Our neighbor fixed the brake line.

At last, a plus, a step forward. Things were looking up, or so it seemed.

That same day, more rain came, the temperature plunged, and the rain turned instantly to ice. Ice on ice. Maybe three inches thick. It was a real killer. Talk about slick. Falling down outside became a regular occurrence for me (Anita and our kids stayed in the house as much as possible.). There was no place to go, anyway. Car wheels spun helplessly in place on the ice. Our familiar world became a foreign, glazed, shining prison, beautiful but deadly.

Christmas came and went, very quietly. With no chance to get out to shop for the holidays, it was a sparse December 25th. Bob Cratchit stuff. It's a good thing we'd bought our turkey early that month. Still, there was lot of grumbling.

We ran out of groceries a couple times during our enforced stay at home. The basics disappeared: potatoes, bread, milk, vegetables, flour, eggs, and the ever popular toilet paper. Also, feed for our livestock. Luckily, our closest neighbor down the road, possessing a four wheel drive vehicle, was able to get to town, and could pick up supplies for us, usually just as happy images of the Donner party started skipping through our desperate, depressed brains.

 date

Nick: One time, after a run to town for groceries, our neighbor stopped in front of our house, and just kept going, sliding on down the road like a sleigh. He finally came to an abrupt halt in a ditch. Luckily, he wasn't hurt. His truck wasn't damaged either. When I headed down the road to help him out, I slipped, and fell hard on the ice, racking up my back really nicely. Which was par for the course, I suppose. Traversing the slick road on foot, it took me about an hour to get all our groceries up to our house. I fell down four more times.

We also ran out of firewood one less than fine day. Which was a surprise to no one. I ended up traversing the ice out to the woods at the back of our property to gather up a supply of wood. This turned into an arctic-style trek, where I got to be both the intrepid explorer and the sled dog. This consisted of pulling a cart loaded to overflowing with fire wood across our frozen field, using nothing but bits of dead grass sticking up through the ice as foot holds. Transporting the cart about 600 feet took about three hours. Needless to say, I spent as much time on my back as I did pulling the cart. But I got the job done.

☙

Cabin fever became a big problem, too. Normally, we tried to get to town at least once a week. We were ice bound on our farm for a full month. We spent a lot of time telling each other we were glad we didn't have a gun in the house — when we weren't arguing over when we'd actually visited Arizona last, or who had purchased the lamp in our dining room. Important stuff.

Finally, the temperature zoomed up to a sweltering 40 degrees, then 50, and the ice began to melt, turning roads and fields and barnyards into thick mud pies. It was a mucky mess, but it was still better than living in the Ice Age.

No one had to tell us this was time to get out and head for town. When we got out to the car, however, we finally noticed the extremely flat tire on the front passenger's side. It wasn't just flat, it was a pancake. We quickly pumped a can of leak repair stuff into the tire, and it quickly swelled up. Then, just as quickly, it proceeded to go flat again. We were going to bring our spare tire into play, but at some time during the long month, it had also gone flat.

We called the auto club for help, but they never came. When we called them again later in the afternoon, they said they'd forgotten about us. They promised to come out the next day. Etcetera ...!

To make a long story a bit shorter, we eventually got to town, and got our lives going again. We should add, though, this wasn't our worst time on the farm — only one of many bad rolls. So, how many straws do you think break a camel's back? You don't really know until you hear the crack. Some camels have stronger backs than others.

Country life is sometimes hell, but it is never dull.

Neighbors

A good neighbor in the country is a resource you can't do without, just like having good fences up for your livestock. Or having $90,000 dollars stashed away in a Swiss bank account. The standoffishness or downright hostility of city neighbor relationships simply won't do. You need someone around, someone outside your family you can depend on. If it's someone who's especially capable and knowledgeable in rural ways, so much the better.

A good neighbor might be there to pull your car out of a ditch or a snow drift. He will not be upset when your ever-roaming goat grazes in his front yard. He may assist with recalcitrant livestock. He'll be happy to furnish you with hay when you suddenly run out, and maybe can't pay anymore for a week or two. Or maybe he'll just loan you some tools you couldn't find anywhere else.

Of course, when you have the chance to return a favor you shouldn't even have to be asked. That's part of the relationship, too. Never make it a one-sided affair. But, if you find a good friend, you'll have your chances to reciprocate. The country will see to that.

☙

Nick: Our good friend J. L. Kimbrough once gave us a hand with transporting some sheep from a farm in Tennessee to our farm in Missouri. J.L. and I drove together. Twelve hundred miles in two days. It was tough going, to say the least. Not only was there the obvious strain of the long haul, but for me there was the added stress of making sure I purchased the best animals possible. If ever there was a time for two people to get on each other's nerves, this was it. But J.L. and I got along fine. Better than when Anita and I go on long trips together. Which is kind of scary. J.L. didn't have to help me, but he was glad to do it; when it was all over, I had to force him to take money for the trip. That's what it's like to have a good country friend.

☙

Good neighbors in the country should be cultivated like a prize crop.

ᘓ

Chapter Four
Systems

"Water, Water Everywhere
(and not a drop to drink)..."

When poet Samuel Taylor Coleridge penned those lines in his *Rime of the Ancient Mariner*, he was talking about seamen stranded on a becalmed ship — surrounded by vast miles of open ocean, but without drinking water. Today in the modern world, we are awash in a sea of rain, rivers, taps, bottles, and fancy jugs of the stuff — water is SO available, SO easy to find, SO prevalent, that we have forgotten how hard it really is to get, keep, and clean it.

When a person begins to think about water — about pipes, and pumps, and electricity, and drilling, and holding tanks, and filters, and bacteria, and agricultural chemicals, and use rates, and flow volumes, and weight-carrying capacity, and distillation standards, and — it's so overwhelming that we're tempted to throw our hands into the air and give up.

But, water is really simple, isn't it? We seem to know instinctively that there is plentiful water in our world, even in desert regions — or, how could anything live there?

Hard to come by, but simple, too... if we can use basic principles, basic practices, basic tools. After all, ancient peoples in the Middle East deserts prospered; they stored infrequent rainwater in vast cistern holding tanks, found sand-covered streams and river oases by looking for the occasional date-palm or green fringe in the dry brown earth, and they did this without benefit of computers, land-mapping satellites, or sophisticated water-seeking radar. They did this by knowing their environment, by building appropriately, and by conserving this precious resource.

"Basic principles, practices, tools..." — and, in today's world, our water resource must be fast, easy and low cost as well. People with scads of cash can build acre-sized ponds, drill deep wells in the desert, and pump using solar arrangements — and although we fervently wish we could join in the spending (!), we're stuck, instead, relying on whatever wits we have, some ability to tinker, and our willingness to experiment and adjust systems to meet our personal needs.

You're probably a lot like us.

You have, most likely, looked at your home or business and recognized a fragility in the system that currently supplies you with water.

This chapter will address these needs, with "fast", "easy" and "low-cost" as primary considerations. Keep in mind there are five steps to water systems... collecting, moving, holding, cleaning, and reusing. You do have to do a certain amount of thinking, adjusting, measuring, and calculating — but you're ready for that. If you weren't ready, you would have skipped this section — you'd just rely on the tap to bring clean water to you forever.

Preliminary Thoughts on Why

So, why DOES a person want to develop a personalized water system? This is a critical question that you must answer before proceeding — the answer will determine how much you spend, how big and functional your system is to be, and, in some detail, how your system works.

Some readers live in areas that face water disruptions on an intermittent basis: Earthquakes, tornadoes, and hurricanes pull down power lines and break water mains — but the region eventually gets repaired. Such a reader may simply want a system that stores usable water for three days to a couple weeks. The original source might well be public taps, channeled through a holding tank that can be isolated and used on its own — or might just be a collection of small containers under the bathroom sink.

On a personal note along that line, from January 1 to January 6, 1999, ice storms ravaged our area. Power was out to almost the entire county for much of that period. We were frozen into our rural home ...and, although we were comfy and cozy with heat, light, and food due to our various "off the grid" backups ...well, our water pump was silenced, and the lines into and throughout the house froze solid. Fortunately, we have "backups for our backups." Bottles and tanks of stored water were pressed into use, and we coped. No showers, no laundry, once-per-day dishwashing, and only one flush allowed in the afternoon for our four-person family ...and, guess what? We only used about 5 gallons per person each day, 20 gallons per day total for all of us (coffee, mixing fruit juices, straight drinking, dishwashing, hair washing and basic hygiene, cooking, and a little bit of clean-ups) ...we survived with minimal discomfort. We knew it was a short-term situation, and used a short-term solution — bottled water. Cheap to set up, easy to use, immediately available in an emergency. Quick to replace.

Had the situation continued for an undetermined time, we would have begun using the backup system of 4,000 gallons of water stored in our cistern — and probably the first thing we would have used water for was a quick shower! Backups for the backups....

Areas that have frequent "boil-water-orders" — that is, significant water contamination in public lines — may want a longer term backup system. If you're on the public tap, and that "b-w order" comes in, you might just switch over to your personal system for a while until the order is removed — three to ten days, typically. Such a water system is more for convenience than for survival insurance, but pays for itself over time in saved energy and decreased anxiety.

Homes that are building new water systems, or that are away from municipal pumps, or for folks who can't afford that new 3,000 foot cased well — your needs are critical and collection and storage will be priorities, even though an emergency isn't part of your immediate picture. Nevertheless, the type of system you set up will often be insulated from emergencies just by virtue of maintaining storage of some kind.

How Much Do You Use?

Let's get down to brass tacks: How much water is enough? If you're a typical individual, you drink about 2 quarts of water per day (including that which is in sodas, coffee and tea, and in juices). Health experts tell us we really should drink more — and some people who are health conscious or who suffer from kidney ailments will drink about twice that amount. If you count all the water used in cooking (boiling and washing foods), you can probably figure that a gallon of water is a pretty conservative figure for an ordinary person's drinking and eating needs. This is at absolute, basic, survival level — no fringe uses.

On average, a single toilet flush consumes 7 gallons of water. Low-flow flushes may be as little as 3 to 5 gallons. The typical person flushes five times per day — about 15 to 35 gallons down the toilet.

One small load of laundry uses up 20 gallons of water for wash and rinse. A large load, 45 gallons.

When you brush your teeth or wash your hands and leave the water running, about a gallon a minute (or more!) goes down the drain.

Taking a shower runs an average of 5 to 7 gallons per minute into the sewers — so a five minute shower uses up 25 to 35 gallons. If you leave the water running for a few minutes to warm up, before getting into the shower — you probably use 50 to 70 gallons for a "quick scrub."

Those are the basic, essential water uses — and the daily total for ONE person to drink, flush, wash a load of laundry and take a shower is:

Low-flow systems: 60 gallons

Normal use: 160 gallons

Here's the typical usage for a household PER DAY:

>   two people: 120-320 gallons
>   three people: 180-480 gallons
>   four people: 240-640 gallons
>   five people: 300-800 gallons
>   six people: 360-960 gallons

Now, let's put these numbers in perspective ...a typical large kitchen trash can holds about 35 gallons. A jumbo trash can, the kind you have to wrestle to the curb, holds about 50 gallons. One person *each day*, uses between one and three *jumbo* trash cans of water. A family of four uses five to twelve *jumbo* trash cans *every day*.

For a week of normal use, a family of four *uses thirty-five to eigthy-two jumbo trash cans filled with water!!* Just try to picture that: up to 82 jumbo trash cans, sitting in your backyard, just to hold the water your family uses for *one week!!*

Kind of mind-boggling, isn't it?

How Much Do You Need?

In good times, we may use a staggering amount of water to keep cool, clean and comfortable — but how much do you really, absolutely *need*? What is the minimum of water you must have to sustain life?

Go back up the preceding list of "use", and you'll find the first item is drinking water ...that's the absolute minimum. If you can put off bathing and washing clothes, you need about a gallon of water per day, per person, to just sustain healthy life. Once again, no fringes.

This is a much more manageable figure: 4 gallons per day for a family of four; 28 gallons per week — about half of a *jumbo* trash can each week, just for drinking and cooking purposes. That's no longer mind-boggling: It's manageable. A four-person family could go for a month on just two jumbo trash cans of water (even if they'd be pretty stinky by then from lack of bathing).

If you double the two jumbo trash cans supply to four-jumbo trash cans, you *would* have water for sponge bathing once or twice a week — and that's still a pretty manageable amount for a month's worth of water for four people.

That's assuming average use ...let's look more carefully at your personal needs for one day:

drinking water:	1 gallon (min)
washing water:	1 gallon (min)
miscellaneous use (fill in)	
_____	___ gallon
_____	___ gallon
_____	___ gallon

X (number of people in household) = _____ gallons daily
X 7 days = _____ gallons per week
X 4 weeks = _____ gallons per month
X 12 months = _____ gallons per year

Remember to include any special needs your family may have for water or liquids — medical issues, special sanitary needs, livestock or pet requirements, and so forth. Consider that my two-adult, two-teenager family used 5 gallons per person daily with only a small compromise in our comfort level ...for a 5 day period.

Even so, over time this could be a VERY LARGE amount of water — if you had to store up a year's worth of water for your family, you'd probably throw your hands up in despair...

Don't.

There are other ways to obtain and maintain water than by digging a giant tank into your back yard... though that would work, too.

With concerns about the safety of municipal water purity, with the anxiety growing about the impact of disasters on water delivery and availability, with individuals who want to "get off the grid" and live a less-complicated life, with folks who want *assurance* that water will be there when they need it, the only answer may be to set up an independent water system.

You want that system to be *simple* to build, *easy* to maintain, the most *reliable* system possible — and you'd like it to be *cheap*, too.

And, if you're concerned about social systems "going bad," you want your water system in place *fast*.

Because we're talking low-cost and fast, we're going to spend time on do-it-yourself projects. We're also assuming that you have some hands-on skills, and are willing to follow directions — but that you will probably adapt whatever system you develop to your own needs. *This is as it should be!* You *must* look closely at your own situation and needs, and plan accordingly — no one else knows your environment and life-style like you do.

Water Basics

A few basics about water:

- Water flows downhill.
- Water can flow uphill *only* if it is pumped or siphoned.
- A pint of water weighs about a pound.
- A gallon of water weighs about 8 pounds.
- A gallon of water is about 1/8 of a cubic foot.
- A cubic foot of water is about 8 gallons.
- A cubic foot of water weighs about 64 pounds.
- A cubic foot of water is 1,728 cubic inches.
- A cubic inch of water weighs about 0.6 ounces.
- Water turns to ice at 32° F and 0° C.
- Ice converts to water at 32° F and 0° C.
- Water, at sea level, boils at 212° F, 100° C.
- Above sea level, boiling requires one added degree for each thousand feet.
- The pumping or pulling weight of water increases in proportion to the depth in a well you go to get it.
- Most hand pumps won't pull water from wells deeper than 200 feet.
- Water mixed with soluble components (such as alcohol or sugar), freeze more slowly at lower temperatures than plain water — and must be hotter before boiling takes place.
- Water *poorly* mixed with soluble components (such as alcohol or sugar) will freeze independently from the components, leaving ice plus sloppy mixture in the container.
- Pure distilled water will not carry electricity (from the lack of ions).

- Water with salt in it will carry electricity quite efficiently.
- Water with sufficient salt in it to "float a potato" is a 10 percent salt solution.
- A person can suffer from "water intoxication" if too much water is consumed, it's a psychological disorder.
- A person can die in three days if no liquids are taken in and weather is hot or the person is very active.
- A cow can easily drink 5 gallons of water each day.
- A goat requires at least 1 gallon of water daily.
- Chickens and rabbits can get by on 5 ounces daily per animal.
- One foot of snow will melt down to 1 inch of water.
- Rain is "soft water" (has no minerals in it).
- Water that boils off and leaves a powdery white residue is "hard water" (has mineral elements dissolved in it).

Collecting

Water comes from only three places: the sky, under ground, and ground surface. This section is going to deal with some fast, low-cost ways for taking water from its place in nature, and gathering it to the place you want it to be. You will notice that there is some overlap in concepts — pumping, for example — that are involved also in "moving" water, but these are small crossovers. You'll notice the applications of these differ, depending on the outcome you're trying to achieve.

All right, one at a time...

Sky Source

Rain, snow, sleet, hail, fog, drizzle, clouds... they are all names for water in its various forms. You've seen basic water collection systems from precipitation from the sky: They're called "puddles"! It's automatic, simple, and requires only two things besides water: a low spot in the ground, and a non-porous surface.

In effect, a garden or livestock pond is the same thing on a grand scale: a concrete lined basin, or a low place in a field that has a clay-like bottom. Ponds are among the most easy-to-construct, most simple water collection systems that exist. A backyard 200-gallon fish pond, pretty small potatoes as far as ponds are concerned, can flush a lot of toilets!

Rainwater Collection

From about 100 degrees longitude (roughly the midpoint of the US) and eastward, there is adequate rainfall to meet the needs of gardens, farms, animals, and human consumption — to the west of that 100 degree division, rainfall is inconsistent, insufficient, or infrequent enough that in order to have enough water, you *must* conserve and collect. In the modern world, the answer to insufficient rainfall has been *well drilling*, which is certainly an option that has been used all over the country. Another option is collection and storage; this is what we'll look at here.

Behind our house, we have a livestock pond. It was here when we moved in. It is situated in a small natural valley between three hills. At the "low" end, a small dike holds the water in, with a rock-covered spillway that can empty during heavy storms into a ravine. The ravine itself leads off at a gradual slope into a river.

The old farmer who decided to put his livestock pond here took advantage of features of the terrain: The pond sits below three gradual and grassy slopes, somewhat like the hollow of a bowl, so that all the rainwater excess flows into the pond. The grassy slopes cover about 5 acres, so there is *a lot* of water flowing into the pond with every rainfall.

That old farmer knew that during heavy rains, the pond would be filled to capacity, and excess would head to the lowest point — it is at that lowest point that he built a spillway... just a slight dip, really... and threw a lot of field rocks over the spot to protect it from being washed out.

The pond dam, the man-made part that actually prevents water from flowing from the hillside directly into the ravine, appears to have been tamped or driven over by tractor or bulldozer, and it has some very large chunks of concrete sticking out of it — looks like old pieces of building foundation. If the dam (the man-made part) at the spillway ever breaks, the water will flow down the ravine and not menace our home, barns, or livestock — another clever piece of planning on our farmer's part.

The pond has been here, perhaps, for forty or fifty years, maybe longer. It holds water, winter or summer, and generations of little minnows have lived there (though it is too shallow to be stocked with game fish). On two banks, good-sized black cherry trees and oaks grow, shading the water during the hottest part of summer.

It holds something like 25,000 gallons of water.

Cost to make it: Assuming ownership of the land, it would run $300 to $600 to have a dozer/tractor scrape the ground, form the dam, and tamp it — it takes about two days.

That's all well and good, but suppose you don't have a piece of farmland, or your land doesn't have the natural gullies and rainfall ours does?

Your house has a roof, with hills and valleys, and the potential to provide useable water. How much? The calculation covers several steps, here's how to find out:

Determine the surface area of your roof: Take one edge of the roof, and multiply it times the edge side (Fig 1). In this hypothetical house, you would multiply 30 x 20 to arrive at a surface area of about 600 square feet.

Figure 1

Figure 2

For a house with odd sizes of walls, as in Figure 2, you can get a rough estimate by adding opposing sides together, then averaging. In our example, 20 + 8 = 28; 20 + 10 = 30. To average, 28 + 30 = 58, then divide by 2 = about 29. To complete the surface area calculation, use your average of wall length, 29, and multiply times the other wall (29 x 20 = 580).

This is your square foot surface area of your roof.

To determine how much water you collect, keep this in mind: A 1 inch rain, if it was all collected, would give you the surface area of your roof times 1 cubic inch of water.

If your roof was 600 square feet, each square foot would give you 12 inches by 12 inches of water, 1 inch deep — or 144 cubic inches of water. Multiply that 144 times the total area (600), and you have the full amount of water, in cubic inches, from your roof: 144 x 600 = 86,400 cubic inches of water.

A gallon is about 77 cubic inches of water — so you could have collected about 1,100 gallons from that one rain. (86,400 divided by 77 = 1,122).

In actuality, you would get somewhat less, because you would allow for rinsing, spillage, and runoff.

But, look what happens if you get a 2 inch rain: 2,200 gallons of water! How about a couple days of steady mild rainfall that adds up to 4 inches? 8,800 gallons.

All you need to complete this water collection picture are: gutters, downspouts and a holding tank.

Holding tank: It can be pretty imposing-sounding... but, really, those "jumbo" trash cans are holding tanks — so is an 18 inch deep $50 kid's wading pool, or a $200 2,500 gallon 36 inch deep by 12 foot wide above-ground "adult" pool. ANYTHING that will hold water can be a "holding tank" ...just remember that if you want to drink that water, you may have to filter or boil it first!

An in-house holding tank — nothing more than an old non-heating water heater — can be plumbed "in line" in most homes with very little adaptation. This will provide an extra 40 to 60 gallons of water at any time there is a disruption in service. If you have city water subject to boil orders and use this kind of tank, just put a shut-off valve between the inflow and the tank, so you can turn off the city water and just use your system.

In rural homes, pumped water may either enter a "pressure tank" — this 40 to 100 gallon metal tank has a rubberized bladder internally. As water fills the tank from an outside source, the bladder deflates and pressure is generated within the tank... so, when you turn on the tap, water flows out readily.

In a slightly more primitive (but still very workable) version, the well pumps water into a holding tank that is set at or slightly above roof level — this becomes a "gravity feed" system that provides plenty of water pressure. Driving through New Mexico on I-40 (a region not noted for its abundant rainfall!), we saw numerous rural houses with roof level water tanks... simple and elegant proof that this system is still in use and still works! Alternatively, a water tank like this could be nothing more elaborate than a jumbo trash can, filled by bucket on a daily basis from the nearby clean river (just be sure to filter or boil your water!).

We mentioned puddles, early on — another simple collection system is just that: a large puddle. Because you want clean water, you would need a collection surface that eliminates loose brush and dirt — here's an idea that costs little, but gets the job done:

Tarp puddle: Look for a natural low spot in your yard. Place plastic sheeting (3 mil thick or thicker, such as you would use for construction) over the low spot. "Seal" the edges by covering with dirt and stomp this down thoroughly — you want as smooth and firm a surface as possible for water to run over. Collection is variable, but can be improved...

Tarp pond: Same supplies as a tarp puddle, but you'll need a shovel or two to enlarge the hole. Even a foot deep, by 4 feet across (a moderate hole that won't take more than a couple hours to dig, even in rough soil) can give you a collection of over 200 gallons of water — especially if you site it beneath a downspout from your roof!

Well, well, well...

Ideally, a deep well is THE primary underground source that provides the most useable, most reliable, most familiar way of acquiring water. In reality, a deep well can cost a small fortune ($2,000 to $8,000) *just to drill* — not including the casing (protective liner), the pump, or the power source. So, we consider instead a not-so-deep well, and plan to filter or boil our drinking water before use...

A shallow well can be anywhere from 8 feet to 25 feet deep. In the olden days, these wells were just dug by hand (watch out for cave-ins!), the inside walls were bricked, and buckets were lowered into the well to draw up the drink.

This system still works. The only modern concerns about this well are: Water may not be available at such a high level in the ground; and ground-water can be badly polluted. But, hey — if you are filtering or boiling your water, the latter problem is solved... so your only concern is how deep to dig.

Alternatively, Lehman's and other companies sell a "hammered well" that you simply bang into the ground until you hit water. This works best in sandy soil, and probably won't work at all if you have to battle with rocks.

Deep Rock company offers a system for home drilling a pumpable well. The cost of the equipment, into the thousands, can be recouped if you are able to drill wells for your neighbors — or if you drill several wells on your own property. The system is fairly easy to operate, and includes a motorized drill that sits at head-height above your intended spot on a pair of stilts. We like the do-it-yourself quality of this system; the problem is you need to already have a water source to help power the drill system. See the Appendix for an address.

Hand pumps for drilled wells run roughly $50 for shallow pumps (to 20 feet) to about $1,500 for pump systems that can pull from 200 feet deep or less. Even Arnold Schwarzenegger couldn't pump strongly enough to pull water from much deeper than 200 feet. Both Lehman's and Kansas Wind Power supply good merchandise (see Appendix), but you may also be able to find a basic system at your local hardware store if you live in the country. Some old cisterns still have hand pumps for bringing the water up (so you don't have to use the bucket-and-rope method!). You can't really kluge together a pump — but you may be able to find a used one more cheaply at farm sales.

On the more costly side, solar-powered pumps and wind driven systems are certainly options. Cost is the primary problem with these approaches — you can expect to pay $3,000 to $10,000 (or more!) to set up a system. Real Goods has whole-house systems and stand alone applications — so does Kansas Wind Power. The water can be drawn up into either a plain holding tank, or a house-feeding pressurized or gravity tank.

All wells need to have "sanitary" protection — this consists of a casing or lining for drilled wells, or a clean shelf or concrete square that covers the ground right up to the edge of the drill hole. This prevents crud from falling down into the system, and possibly causing illness. If you decide to go with a dug well, be sure to bring your "brickwork" up three feet or so above ground, and place a sturdy cover over the well opening that *can only be lifted by adults.* A combination lock wouldn't hurt matters, either. This is done both to protect the cleanliness of the water (cats and chickens will fall in), and because little kids find these things just too fascinating — and a plunge into cold water from 10 or 20 feet can be a life-threatening experience for a little one.

Streams and Rivers

You've seen this in Western movies; in films about abject poverty; and in glimpses from rural areas — Ma and the kids down at the river, scooping water with wooden pails. Guess what? That system *still* works just fine — with the exception that today's Ma probably uses 5 gallon plastic buckets, and totes her pails in a garden cart.

If today's Ma is clever, she'll wade into that stream and only collect the fastest-moving water in her buckets — avoiding entirely the muddy bank waters.

But if Ma is *really* smart, she might rig up a length of 4 inch PVC pipe so that one end sits in the middle of the stream at a slight waterfall, collecting water — and the other end slopes down to feed her buckets directly.

Suppose that Pa wants to make things a little easier on Ma — he buys (or welds together) a "ram pump" — a device known for hundreds of years. A ram pump uses the movement of water in a pipe down a slope (the "drop" of the water), to force air into a small chamber. The water is channeled into another pipe, and the air in the chamber can be used to force the water *uphill.* It may take several rams in series to bring water up a steep hill to the house — or, if the house isn't too far above the river, a single one may do the trick. Pa and Ma will probably spend $1,200 for the pump and for all the extra piping if they go this route (Lehman's and Kansas City Wind Power are sources).

Cleaning and Filtering

Surface water — bubbling brooks, streams, and rushing rivers — are all excellent water sources, with an important caveat: The water *is not clean!!!* It *will* be loaded with bacteria, critter poop, dead bugs, fish bits, and other assorted goodies. Even the most pristine high country flow coming off a glacier is loaded with things that can make you sicker than sick.

IT MUST BE BOILED AND/OR FILTERED!!!

Even if your brother-in-law drank all last summer directly from the stream near his home, *you must not do it!!!* Your B-I-L may have developed some immunity to his local bacteria, but you haven't, your spouse hasn't, and your kids certainly haven't. You and the spouse might survive the severe bloody diarrhea, cramps, and dehydration — but your kids probably won't.

Boil and filter. Boil and filter. Make it your stream water mantra.

Boiling for ten minutes will destroy most bacteria — that's a rolling boil for ten minutes, mind you. However, boiling will not remove chemicals or other pollutants...for that you need a filter designed specifically (and you must read filter labels) to see which ones claim to eliminate chlorine, heavy metals, and so on. Filters can be "in line" (situated in your plumbing so that water automatically passes through), or free-standing on your countertop... it makes no difference, as long as you use it! There are numerous makes and varieties of filters (including Katadyn, Pur, and Terra Cotta), and each has different filtering capabilities — some only provide "good tasting water," without removing bacteria or other pollutants. Each filtering element will probably have to be replaced after a certain period of time. You must read the specifications, and decide what fits your situation. Better filters cost significantly more. Keep extra filter elements on hand.

If you are utterly certain that local agriculture chemicals or other pollutants are not present in the water (glacier melt probably is a fairly low-chemical pollutant source), then boiling and cloth filtering may be sufficient.

Cloth filtering is basically what takes place when you use a coffee filter — water and big molecules can pass through, but dirt and debris are left behind. Use cheesecloth, folded, or cut up a clean (boiled and dried) sheet and use that.

Reuse

One of our early experiments in water use included collecting used water from our sinks and supplying that to the garden area. This collecting and reusing "dirty" water is called "greywater" — and that's generally what it looks like. Gathered from sinks in kitchen and bathroom(s), this water will contain some dissolved soaps and detergents, dirt, food bits, and assorted things we might wash off of our hands. It's pretty unappetizing looking.

But! It's also perfectly suitable for watering fruit trees, flowers, and around the bases of garden plants. It's better not to get greywater on leaves of lettuce or other leafy greens, and on fruits... you don't want to eat this stuff.

Collection of greywater can be by pipe — just plumb the house so greywater drains into an outside tank, then run a hose from the tank to wherever you want it. Or, use the simplest, most low-cost method: remove pipes from under your sinks, and put a 5 gallon bucket in their place. Empty or replace when 2/3 full.

There are some innovators who are looking for ways to further use greywater — by some limited filtering and cleaning (many modern soaps break down readily in sunlight), it *may* be reusable for raising pond fish, or watering livestock, or flushing, or even washing clothing, but *not* for drinking or dishwashing. In regions where good, steady, clean supplies of water are limited, this is certainly an option for extending your supplies.

So...

Water is crucial to survival. We've made it hard, in this modern age, to understand the simple value of water — even though we might guide and channel it for thousands of miles just to get a green front lawn.

We know that we can certainly live comfortably with much less water than we currently use — we could even use Great-Grandma's simple method: a pitcher and a basin, to limit water use, instead of leaving the tap running while brushing our teeth. We know that we can use water more efficiently and more productively.

All we have to do, on the farm, is put that knowledge to work.

Septic Systems

Let's talk about something really, really gross. Septic systems. Actually, to the point, the day our septic system failed. Actually, it didn't fail all at once. It was more of a gradual death. These things happen. We knew something was pretty much wrong when everything we flushed down our toilet started coming up in our bathtub. Which didn't much inspire anyone to want to take baths or showers.

Point of fact: Septic tanks are little worlds unto themselves, and they depend on a balance of water and waste and healthy bacteria to keep things running smoothly. When something goes wacky in this equation, the system will often go haywire. What happened in ours was the bacteria were weakened by too much bleach dumping down the toilet. This caused a lapse in the breakdown of waste, which caused a hard crust to form over the sludge. This meant no water could get into the system, causing the backup into our bath tub.

Simple.

But not good.

☃

Nick: My first job was to dig down to where the septic tank was located. This was after ascertaining that to have this problem fixed by professional sources would cost more than $500! At this, there was no doubt at all who would get to do the work.

Before I knew what I was doing (a big mistake), I dug down to the tank, and replaced some pipes leading from the house, thinking this would help. It didn't. In fact, not fixing the problem properly only made it worse. At one point, after I'd re-buried the tank, the pressure inside grew so strong, it ruptured a seam in a pipe I'd put in, creating an upward gush of flushed material right through the dirt, kind of a poop volcano.

After that, I made it a point to avoid the hit or miss approach to fixing the problem. I opened up the septic tank itself, and found out what the problem really was.

At first, I thought I might have to clean out the entire tank by hand, which I tried to do. But this would have taken about a hundred years, so I gave up on that. Instead, I worked on breaking up the built-up crust I discovered, and bringing the tank bacteria population back to life (so that it could do what it had to do).

Maybe the worst part of this task was the odor, which, if you got it on you — and there was no way around that — never went away, except by wearing off with time.

❧

I spent four days on this job. My wife wouldn't let me come in the house until I'd taken off all my clothes, which needed immediate washing. And I still smelled.

This time I managed to correct the problem. But I certainly could have found better ways to use my time.

The lesson to be learned here is that having a farm septic tank is not like living in the city, where everything just empties into a sewer, and is forgotten. When you have your own waste disposal system, you have to act with thought, and a sense of responsibility. Or else! It's just another chunk of living in the country no one really wants to talk about.

You never do get used to the smell, you know.

Doing Without Electricity

Some people think that living without electricity is somehow romantic. A kind of nineteenth century dream, a return to simplicity. Thoreau and all that stuff. That's okay, but we're not sure if this is a complete picture. If you decide to try this lifestyle, you should consider all the ramifications of living without electricity. Get it right!

We lived for three full years without electricity, to see if we could. And we did. Successfully, from 1991 to 1994.

But what did this move entail?

Well, to begin with, everything we did revolved around the basics of life, and around the idea that we didn't have electricity to back us up. There was little progress in terms of moving life into new areas. Everything we did basically was a holding action. The simplest things became long chores. For instance, a straightforward thing like flushing the toilet meant walking outside to our rain water barrels, and hauling in buckets of water, as opposed to pushing down a handle. We found out just how much water and energy it really took to accomplish a flush. But, so what? Instead of just freezing food, all perishables had to be canned or dried right away. Moreover, there was no forgiveness in this lifestyle. If we forgot to make candles, we sat in the dark at night. If we didn't process our food, it spoiled.

At night, we did everything by candlelight and lamplight. We read books to our kids by candlelight every evening, which was an enjoyable family moment. But, to be honest, this is probably why we can't read anything without glasses now.

Every thought revolved around the reality of no electricity. This made us super efficient with our time and actions. To be totally focused on one's actions makes for super self-awareness, but it is also very tiring. After a bit, you need a rest, a distraction. Or you simply burn out.

After the three years were up, we knew we could live without electricity, so, without any fanfare, we had the electricity turned back on, and got on with living in the twentieth century.

So, what exactly did we accomplish by putting ourselves through this particular adventure? For one thing, we learned a lot about ourselves. We saw what we could actually do when pushed to the wall. We also got a sense of reality undistorted by the conveniences of the modern world. Also, Anita ended up writing a successful book about the subject: *How to Live Without Electricity — And Like It,* (Breakout Productions, 1997). So, we actually made money off having no electricity.

Which only goes to show, you never know where a particular decision might take you.

Of course, just because you might decide to go off the grid, that doesn't mean you have to meet the world without any electricity. There are generators: gas or diesel powered, wind powered, and solar powered. Personally, we think solar is the best approach to self-power, mainly because it is a totally renewable resource. There's always sun — except at night, of course. It is expensive to start up, but once you have your system in place, you are set. You can also work with small rechargeable and renewable batteries for radios, flashlights, and the like.

One word about using gas generators: It's a mistake to think if you have one that it's going to be there for you twenty-four hours a day. That just ain't so. Besides, no matter how good they are, the more you use them, the faster they wear out. Also, buy cheap, and you buy disappointment. The only good gas generators — ones to bet your life on — cost money. Remember, when they break, you have nothing.

Also, don't cut any of those electrical wires in your house. Burning bridges is always a mistake. We can say this, because we did just that. We did some house renovation when our electricity was off, and we cut numerous wires, thinking what the heck, we're not going to be messing with this junk any more. We were pretty indiscriminate So, we got to learn all about electrical wiring later on when we had to patch up our electrical lines. Keep your options open.

Be sure of what you want to do. Don't be swayed by silly thoughts of romance. Know what you want to get out of your nonelectric experience. One idea would be to turn off your electricity at your breaker box for a month to see how it goes. Then decide.

We read letters in various rural-oriented magazines all the time from folks who are champing at the bit to get off the grid. Some seem to want to be self-sufficient. Some take the rejection of electricity as a sign of nobility. Some think it will bring their family together. Some just plain hate the modern era. Be careful about your electrical decisions, about what you're rejecting, and just how it'll impact your life to be without power. There can be much stress involved with living without electricity. Will you like it? Only you can answer that question. But don't do it thinking that it will somehow fix all your problems. To the contrary, you'd better have a pretty strong family relationship when you get into this deal. Approaching the no power life from the wrong angle could very easily make it one of those last straws.

Heating and Cooking With Wood

There is something especially comforting about wood heat.

So, you think cooking and heating with wood is neat. Well, it can be, once you get the hang of it, and you have a decent stove. That's the trick.

The process of starting fires in a wood stove — cooking or heating — may seem pretty straightforward, and it can be. You start with a match, right? Well it's a bit more complicated than that. You can find many books that will give you someone's version of kindling a blaze. We tried most of the traditional ones, and failed miserably with them. You may end up trying them, too, before you hit on the method that works consistently for you, which may be somewhat improvised to fit your situation. Just avoid any recipe that starts off, "Take 1 gallon of gasoline..." — unless you want to end up featured in a "dumb-guy" story at your local hospital.

One of the most important traits for learning to build fires is patience. Don't be in a hurry or get angry. Losing your cool will only get in the way of the process. You also need to be consistent once you find what works for you. Trying to cut corners may take a job that usually lasts a minute or two and turn it into an hour's worth of grumbling and frustration. On winter mornings, when your house temperature may be down to 35 degrees, you do not want this to happen.

Now, let's get to your wood stove — heating or cooking, it doesn't matter. Just make sure it's a good one. A badly sealed stove, or one that's rusty, will be a constant source of irritation for you, as it will most certainly leak smoke. This warning refers to most old stoves you will encounter. We had an old cook stove in our kitchen — it must have been seventy years old — that was well beyond the end of its life. But we stretched it for a few years more. Consequently, we had a saying that was a part of this experience: "Wind from the south, smoke in your mouth." Basically, when the wind came from a southerly direction, the stove backpuffed and leaked.

When the wind came from the north, everything was fine. The stove was great then. But, as you might guess, the wind wasn't always from the north.

We love wood heat. There is something especially comforting and satisfying about it. But there are a number of factors, drawbacks, to think about before you decide to go this route. To begin with, wood heat is not constant; sometimes it may be too hot, other times, too cool for your taste. Even when you get the hang of tending a fire in a general way, the wood you're using — age and quality — can throw off the outcome. Then, there's the matter of having to keep the fire stoked. If you don't pay attention to this the fire will go out, and you'll have to start the procedure all over again. Wood fires, then, are like small children: they have to be watched all the time. Too, burning firewood means you can run out of it, so there's a never-ending cycle of replenishing your supply that becomes part of your daily, weekly, or monthly life. And, believe me, no matter how much firewood you collect, unless you keep on top of the situation constantly, you do run out. There's nothing like staring at a dwindling wood pile with the knowledge that a snowstorm is hours away to add stress to your life. On the other side of the weather coin, using wood cooking during the summer, when your kitchen might be 90 degrees anyway, becomes a less than appealing activity. We had a small propane stove we used during the summer months (we resigned ourselves to little or no baked foods for that time period).

Of course, you can't think too much about the safety angle regarding wood stoves. Wood stoves cause house fires. That is a fact. You have to inspect and clean those chimneys and stove pipes periodically, or you can end up with a build-up of creosote which, if ignited, can generate heat up to 2,000 degrees, which will do nothing positive for your home. You also need to check your chimney for cracks, and for any deterioration of your various insulation points. You can't forget to do these things, or take your system for granted, no matter how simple it may seem. One flaw can burn your house down.

Then, you must be mindful of how big you build your fires. You can't build all-day or all-night blazes. These will burn your house down as well as any other method.

Plus, there's the matter of procuring firewood. You can buy it, which gets to be expensive after a while; or you can collect your own. This means cutting wood. You can use axes and handsaws, but this takes forever, and will drain every ounce of living energy you possess from your body, especially if you are not used to extended, demanding, physical activity. Your only real alternative is learning to use a chain saw, which is a very daunting pastime. Chain saws are very efficient, but they are also very dangerous. They cut off fingers, and create large, gaping slices in any body parts they touch. This is a fact of chain saws, and you can never become complacent with them — unless you really like nicknames like Stumpy and Three Finger.

Nor can we forget about splitting firewood. It takes both endurance and coordination. You need to have a sense of distance and a good, flowing swing of your maul or ax from the shoulders. You might be splitting pieces of wood, for instance, that are no more than 4 inches in diameter. That takes a good aim, which must be as instinctive as it is measured. You don't want to spend all your time chopping up the ground around your wood pieces.

ᘓ

Nick: I've always enjoyed splitting wood myself, but it can be dangerous. I've heard stories of people splitting wood who've cut off parts of a foot, or gashed themselves badly in the leg with a single glancing blow off a piece of wood. I was splitting wood when I ruptured a disk in my back.

ଔ

So, you imagined by going to wood heat and cooking, you were taking a step toward simplifying your life. Think again. This is a decision that takes both determination and thought.

Like most aspects of country living.

ଔ

ॐ

Chapter Five
Ensuring Your Food's Future

We have taken it for granted for so long that food will "just be there" that we have made ourselves subject to any breakdown in the chain of food production and delivery. You can avoid being a victim of the system by growing your own food.

We who have lived during the latter twentieth century in America have unknowingly experienced something our ancestors would have thought of as Eden: plentiful, varied, nutritious food, available for only small amounts of money.

Why, any one of us can purchase about 100 hearty meals, made from pinto beans and rice, for less than $25, if we so choose — or we can dine on individual meals of alligator, emu, lion, buffalo, or other exotic meats for about the same amount. We can find fresh, crisp greens and flawless fruit on any day of the year within just a few miles at the nearest supermarket.

Even for the very poorest in our country, special programs make it possible to acquire plentiful foods of a nutritious nature. It is *so* easy to get food in this country, that our nation's poor are among the fattest people in the world. The greatest food problem this country faces isn't hunger — it's obesity!

Even so, drowning in this glorious overabundance, the average American has no idea, *no idea*, where food comes from, how it gets to the store, or how the entire food system operates. The "seed —> soil —> growth —> harvest —> storage —> shipping —>preparing —>market —> consumer" chain has been forgotten. We have taken it for granted for so long that food will "just be there" that we have made ourselves subject to any breakdown in the chain of food production and delivery. We have made potential victims of ourselves.

We have accepted the business norm of "just-in-time" delivery — JIT. JIT is a process that allows retail stores to maintain only enough inventory to fill their shelves — as the shelves are picked over by shoppers, special computer systems in the cash registers record what item was purchased — you've seen the list on your register receipts. An order is then sent automatically, by that same computer system, to the company that makes the product, and a shipment is prepared.

Typically, shipments of new shelf items are received three or four times a week — so the shelves always look full.

The problem is thanks to JIT, there's nothing in storage in the back rooms anymore. There isn't even a warehouse attached to the store. Don't believe it? Ask to use your supermarket's restroom ...they're usually in the back where the storage used to be. Count the pallets there — prepare to be shocked.

Should delivery cease for a mere seven days, shelves would be bare. If icy roads, earthquake or civil disruption suspended trucking for a month, the store would be utterly empty — and people would be mighty upset. Upset, you see, because they assumed that since food has "just been there" it would "ALWAYS be there".

In the country, one of the earliest things you notice is that you can't grow all the foods you want all year around. You can't even grow some of your favorite foods — say, oranges or bananas or chocolate at all (except maybe in Hawaii or Southern California or the southern end of Florida).

Because you can't grow a zucchini in snow, you quickly learn about the concept of stocking up. In essence, you provide your own food inventory, held in your own food warehouse (pantry), that ideally suits your own needs. More details about this can be found in Anita's book, *How to Develop a Low-Cost Family Food Storage System* (Breakout Productions, 1995).

You can stock up by shopping supermarket sales, by acquiring instant military meals or by growing your own food in a home garden. By far the cheapest method for getting good, wholesome, perfectly fresh food is from your garden.

Your garden begins with SEEDS.

Have you ever experienced the horror of "seed shock?" That's the reaction of many gardeners to the cost of vegetable seeds these days. Whether you're perusing catalogs or checking seed packs in a local store, prices for these garden starters seem to have hit new highs. Some we've noted: $2.19 for 1.5 *grams* of leek seed (a gram is 1/28 of an ounce); $1.95 for 500 *milligrams* of zinnia seed (500 milligrams is half of a gram, or about 1/50 of an ounce); and $2.45 for 20 pumpkin seeds — you know, just exactly like the hundreds you find inside those Halloween pumpkins, the ones that get thrown away when you're making a jack-o-lantern for the kids.

At these rates, a pound of any type of seed sells for roughly the cost of an equal weight of gold...

You can just about eliminate this annual seed expense by obtaining seeds from your own plants. Though some sources may lead you to believe that seed saving is some esoteric agricultural process, concealed from we mere mortals, keeping seeds is really as straightforward as gardening itself. It doesn't take a rocket scientist — just a modicum of attention to detail and careful handling.

By saving your own seeds, you will save a bundle in hard-earned cash over buying seeds annually — you'll assure your ability to keep producing food for yourself and your family (and friends), no matter what goes on in the rest of the world — and you'll develop food plants that are literally adapted to do well in *your* backyard, specifically adapted to the way you garden, to your weather, and to your garden conditions. As a bonus, you'll be perpetuating living history, as we'll see later.

Begin next year's garden this year, by selecting the plants that will provide your seeds. Pass by the hybrids, no matter how much you may prefer these types of plant. A hybrid is the product of a selective crossing of two (or more) unrelated strains of a plant; say, a variety of tomato that develops a thick, strong stem might be crossed with a type that produced extra-large fruit. The resulting first-generation (or "F1") offspring will display the best traits of both parent plants. Hybrids are generally more vigorous than either parent, which is quite desirable!

Seeds from these hybrids, however, will not produce true to type. The new plants will "revert" to something like the parents, or possibly like an ancestor of one or both of the parents. In the case of tomatoes, the seed of hybrid fruit often reverts to a cherry tomato-type ancestor.

Instead, save seeds only from open pollinated (also called "non-hybrid") plants. OPs aren't as common in seed catalogs as they were a decade ago, but they're frequently available as "old favorites" or "heirloom" plants — "Golden Bantam" corn and "Rutgers" tomato, for example. OP seeds reproduce true to type year after year, given a little help and wise guidance from their gardener. When reading seed descriptions or packs, hybrid plants, by law, must be labeled as hybrids — sometimes only as "F1." So if it doesn't say, "hybrid" or "F1," it's probably OP.

A few OP varieties are self-pollinating, with individual flowers on the plant providing their own genetic material. These include beans, lettuce, peas, and tomatoes. This means you can grow several varieties of each— for example, Romano, Kentucky Pole, and Wax beans — in the same garden, and the plants will not crossbreed.

Other common OP plants produce seed through pollination either by breezes or by insects. These include corn, beets, cabbages, and other brassicas, carrots, melons, cucumber, radishes, spinach, squash, pumpkins, and turnips. For such types you have three options to prevent accidental crossing.

(1) You can plant only a single representative of the group;

(2) You can stagger plantings so that seeds of crossable types mature at different times (our preference); or

(3) You can hand-pollinate and hand-protect the individual plants that have been selected to produce seeds.

There is a fourth option that may appeal to the adventurous: letting plants of a particular type cross freely. For example, you could plant in proximity two types of cucumber — an 8-inch slicing variety and a tiny, prickly gherkin. The next year's harvest from your own F1 cross could be very disappointing — or you could produce a truly desirable and tasty new vegetable!

Keep only seeds from plants that have done particularly well in your garden: those that are resistant to local insects and weather conditions and that have the best-tasting fruit. After several years of saving seeds from your own "line," you will have developed plants uniquely and individually adapted to your needs.

Store saved seeds in glass jars with tightly fitting lids and keep them cool. There is some controversy about freezing seeds — some people swear by it, others say it ruins the viability (ability to grow) of the seeds. We've done both, and can't say that we've seen a noticeable difference either way — after all, many seeds can overwinter directly in the ground in your garden, without any harm at all ...you know, because you find all those "volunteer" sprouts the next spring!

Make labels for every seed type, and keep the labels inside the jars — otherwise, you risk having the label fall off in storage, and end up with an unknown collection. Include on the label the year of harvest, and the specific variety (that is, "1999, Longkeeper Tomato") and any interesting traits of growth that might help you in the future.

Seeds stored in cool to freezing temperatures should remain viable for several years (although lettuce and spinach like replanting every year). It's not unusual, though, to find that only half a batch of home-collected seeds will grow, so always keep more than you expect to need. It's a good practice to plant at least some of your stored seed every year, to keep supplies fresh. But *never* plant all the seed of one type — if there is an unexpected crop failure, you won't have any left to fall back on.

Generally, when you are harvesting the garden to eat the results, you are picking the fruit before the seeds-to-be are mature and ready for saving. When you save fruit for seed, you need to allow it to reach its ripest condition before picking, which is *way* past the point where the fruit tastes good anymore. The optimum condition for saving the seed of both **annuals** (plants that produce seed during the first year) and **biennials** (plants that require two year's growth to produce seeds) follow:

Annuals

Beans: Allow the very first 20 to 30 pods (or more) on your green beans to hang on the plant until dry (or close to dry, if your weather is humid). Mark these pods with yarn or by other means so that you know which they are. Pick and allow pods to finish drying indoors or undercover. Shell and save.

Or, if you are producing field beans such as pintos or great northerns, pick your early beans freely — eat them like green beans — until late in the season. Let the last pods dry while they're still hanging on the plants. If the weather is too damp and the seeds begin to mildew, pull the entire plants by the roots and hang them upside down in a sheltered area until the pods are completely dry. Crack out the seeds, and store them in glass jars with tight lids. Some folks add a bay leaf per jar to repel bugs.

Corn: Plant only a single variety, or stagger plantings so that the varieties mature at different times. Serious corn growers advocate saving seeds from no less than 100 ears, so that a number of different plants are represented in your genetic seed stocks. But it's better to save seed from just a few ears than to not save any at all — choose seeds from widely spaced plants to allow greater diversity. Select only cobs that represent the best of your corn: hardy plants, strong and upright in the wind — or able to stand upright again after being blown over; ears filled out; little or no insect damage; husky kernels. Let the corn dry in the husk while still on the plant. If the weather is damp and there's a risk of mildew, bring the husks indoors. When thoroughly dry, remove the husks and hang the cobs to complete drying until the kernels are slightly loose. Shell and store.

Cantaloupes: There are many varieties of these aromatic melons, including the familiar orange-fleshed supermarket type, green-fleshed muskmelons, and even a small, hardy indigenous North American sort called "mango melon" or "vine peach." These all cross freely. See the section on pumpkins for information on hand-pollination. Select several early fruits to eat from these plants. When *very* ripe, remove the seeds, rinse them (generally, viable seeds sink and "empties" float), and dry on a plate before storing.

Cucumbers: If you have several plants, save the seeds from the first fruit on one and the last fruit from another. If you have just one plant, you'll have to save seed from the last fruits, for if the cukes aren't picked, the plant will stop bearing. Let a couple of large, healthy cukes remain on the vine until the fruit has turned a golden color. Peel and gently mash the whole cucumber — or at least remove the seed cavity. Put this in cool water and let stand at room temperature for several days; it will become pretty smelly. Pour off the liquid as well as the goo floating in the water. Viable seeds will have settled to the bottom of the container. Rinse in clean water, spread the seeds on a plate to dry before storing them.

Peas: Treat the same as beans.

Pumpkins, Winter & Summer Squash: These all come from four species of the *Cucurbita* genus. Crossing within species is possible, so you should plant only one variety from each one, or stagger your plantings, or space widely apart. *Cucurbita pepo* includes acorn, cocozelle, crookneck, scallop, pumpkins and zucchini. *Cucurbita maxima* includes banana, hubbard, buttercup and turban squash. *C. moschata* covers butternut and "cheese" squash. And *C. mixta* includes cushaws. So you could confidently plant an acorn squash, a hubbard squash, and a butternut squash in the same patch without any fear of crossbreeding.

Suppose, though, you want to grow pumpkins and zucchini, both members of the *C. pepo* group. Then what? Well, you could separate the plantings by several hundred feet, which will slow down pollination by insects. Or you could hand-pollinate female flowers. To do this you detach a male flower (it will have a slender base), and carefully tear away the flower petals so that only the long central pollen-bearing anthers and stem remain. Gently swab this across the newly opened female flower (with tiny bulge of fruit at its base), to distribute pollen. Use several male flowers on each female. Gently tape the female flower shut, and you're done.

If the *Cucurbita* species cross and produce fruits, the results will be perfectly edible and often quite interesting — another F1 home-grown hybrid.

Potatoes: These are fascinating plants. Saving "seed" can be as simple as storing whole potatoes from this year's crop over the winter, either in a cool location or heavily mulched right in the garden. In the spring, just plant the sprouted tubers.

Or, you can save actual potato seeds: your own hybrids, again. For this, select at least three different varieties with similar growing periods — for example, three "long-season" potatoes. Form mounds, or "hills," as planting sites, then plant each hill with all three types. Plants will flower and cross readily, and will produce their regular tubers as well as tiny tomato-like fruit near the plant tops. Don't eat these tiny fruits, but save the seeds from them. The next year, plant the seeds as you would tomato seeds. The resulting tubers, hybrids of the original varieties planted, may be wonderful or may be insipid. This second generation won't, however, produce seed — but you can save the best tubers to carry on your own hybrid line, assuming it's a good one.

Radishes: Radishes cross readily, so plant only one variety at a time. Leave several radishes in the ground after you harvest. As the weather warms, these should send up long seed stalks, which may require staking to prevent breaking. Collect the seeds when those inside the pods rattle freely. Store as usual.

Spinach: Varieties of spinach cross easily, and the pollen can be carried long distances on the wind. As the weather warms, watch for the plants that go to seed *last* — selecting these will increase the length of your growing season in future years. Save several of these plants, allowing them to send up seed stalks. Harvest the seed when it's dry, and store it as usual.

Tomatoes: The varieties seldom cross unless plants are growing intertwined or are pollinated by hand. Pick the selected fruit after it has become *very* ripe on the vine. Mash it, and treat it as described for cucumbers. Then, wash the seed and spread it on a plate to dry before storing.

Watermelons: Pollinated by insects, so follow precautions to prevent crossing such as separating plants, hand-pollination (see Pumpkin section), or stagger plantings. Seed can be saved from fully ripe or overripe fruit. Collect ripe, black seeds either by mashing the fruit as you would cucumbers or simply by saving them after the melon is eaten. Dry on a plate before storing.

Biennials

Beets: Grow only one variety each year (say, Ruby Queen), since beets are wind-pollinated. Store fully mature beets in sand in a root cellar or heavily mulch plants that are left in the garden over winter. The stored beets should be planted in early spring. Beets will send up a long seed stalk and produce bunches of seeds. When the top begins to look dry, pull the entire plant and hang it under shelter. As it dries further, seeds may fall loose, so you'll need to either sweep them up daily or fasten a paper bag around the stalk to catch them. Store.

Cabbage and other brassicas: This large family includes kale, kohlrabi, broccoli, cauliflower, brocco-flower, and Brussels sprouts as well as cabbage. These all cross freely, so predictable seeds are produced only when cross-breeding precautions are followed. Crosses are edible, but you won't know what you'll get. As with beets, select the most disease-resistant and firm fruits, and either store them under cool conditions or mulch them heavily in the garden over winter. Plants send up a seed stalk, which may require support. Pick the stems when they begin to dry, and hang under shelter to complete the process. Collect seeds and store.

Carrots: Varieties cross, and domestic carrots also cross with their wild relative Queen Anne's lace. To keep your lines pure, you'll need to remove all the wild plants from several hundred feet around the garden. Store carrot roots over the winter and replant at early spring as you would beets. Shake the seeds loose from the heads and store.

Onions: They are pollinated by insects, so it's best to keep only a single variety. Save large, insect-resistant bulbs over the winter as you would beets. In spring the plants send up a tall, pretty blossom stock. Before the stalks fall, harvest the tiny black seeds. The stalks may also be hung to dry.

Turnips and Rutabagas: Treat as described for beets. Save only the best.

Seeds represent the lives and tastes of our ancestors — the food that nourished them being carefully handed down to us through all those men and women saving their own seeds. There are literally thousands of plant varieties around that are nearly invisible, unless you look for them. Perhaps a neighbor has a special tomato she has grown for decades; perhaps a relative keeps growing a favorite bean, handed to him by an older relative, who emigrated from Eastern Europe with a handful of seeds in his pocket. You'll seldom find these seeds in catalogs, and occasionally "Uncle Charlie's watermelon" may be the only example of that type *anywhere*.

The "Brandywine" tomato is one of these homestead seeds. Reportedly perpetuated by Amish and Mennonite families, this tomato has finally been seen in seed catalogs in the past few years. It grows on a "potato-leaf" plant, and produces what is universally acknowledged to be among the finest tasting of all tomatoes. The flavor is spicy, fruity, winey, and as unlike supermarket tomatoes as you can imagine. Brandywine is also very thin-skinned and must be eaten right after it ripens. Because they cannot be shipped like commercial tomatoes, they simply wouldn't exist if families didn't continue to propagate them.

Another example is the "Winter King and Queen Watermelon." Watermelons originated in Africa, but this variety is said to be a favorite of desert-living Native Americans, who have kept it going for its exceptional storage qualities. It is round, pale green, weighs about 10 pounds at maturity, and will keep for months on the shelf. But it is so crisp and thin-skinned that it cannot be shipped — sudden movement can split the rind easily. If its seeds are not saved, this melon will die out just as surely as did the dodo and passenger pigeon.

If you would like to start saving your own seed — or to grow a piece of living history — try querying your gardening friends about the varieties that have pleased them and done well for them. You can also contact the Seed Saver's Exchange (RR 2, Box 239, Decorah, IA 52101), an organization dedicated to preserving old and forgotten varieties of plants. The annual membership fee allows you to request any type of seed from other members, just for the cost of postage.

Finally, if you want to compute the value of your seeds, you can do it one of two ways:

(1) Figure out how much food you can grow with those seeds, and determine the market price of the food.

(2) Weigh your seeds and multiply times the price of gold (check your newspaper's business section).

Either way, you can see that your seeds are truly "worth their weight in gold!"

Organics

We think organic gardening is great. The food tastes better than chemically grown produce, and it's better for you. But there's a catch when you start growing it: You can't be totally organic if you don't prepare for it first.

We've known numerous disillusioned folks who began organic, and gave up when the bugs took over, in spite of their use of all the organic-oriented remedies. They ended up becoming rabid chemical-dumping sinks. People have said to us more than once, "I'd rather eat chemically produced tomatoes than feed everything I grow to bugs." It's frustrating, to say the least.

Where did these individuals go wrong?

At the bottom line, they probably didn't bother to think about the soil. You can't be organic just because you want to be. You have to make it happen. If the soil on your newly acquired property has been depleted of nutrients for years, for whatever reason, going organic immediately is plant suicide. We found you may have to give up the idea of establishing a garden in a particular area for a year or two while you coax the soil back to health with compost and lime, or whatever. You may not like it, but it's better than working hard all spring and summer on a garden only to end up with a handful of pale, gnarled green beans and stunted wormy ears of corn.

You can't trick Nature!

The Real Country Kitchen

Having had the privilege of spending time in a number of true, working, country kitchens, there is only one critical thing that they all have in common:

Not one looks like the "country kitchen" motif in decorating magazines.

Attractive baskets and fancy teapots do not fill every nook and cranny. Very few "working" kitchens have clean, pretty wallpaper — or any wallpaper at all. More often, the walls are painted in light colors. The faucets aren't gold, brass, or even expensive. The stove looks sturdy and practical, without grills, gadgets, or extra dials... sometimes it's a wood cooker. There aren't many visible "handy helper" do-dads like food processors around. Vegetables and fruit do not sit in attractive wire baskets on ledges, and grand bouquets of exotic flowers do not adorn nook tables.

What you will see, in the most efficient of these *real* country kitchens: abundant space on counters, tables, and ranges. The most precious commodity is *space*. The more you have, the better — you need space to have room to prepare that lamb carcass for the freezer, space for your canning jars to cool while you start the next batch, space to stack the dishes after a big meal. When everybody comes over for a buffet, that space is given over to plates and bowls and dishes of everyone's favorite foodstuff.

When you open cupboards, you'll find them stacked and filled with canned goods, cereals, and spices. This is the first-level storage system, the place where the day-to-day supplies are visible and handy. Take down a can of cranberry sauce, and tomorrow a similar can from the more distant pantry will fill that spot — it, in turn, to be replaced by a can from the supermarket next weekend. Somewhere around the pickling spices, you'll find the canning jar lids — conveniently together since last summer's preserving. There's a package of birthday candles, some strike-anywhere matches, and two kinds of vinegar up there, too.

You'll also find mismatched tableware — enough plates for the folks, the kids, the grandkids, and a few cousins. They're mismatched because, over time, the various sets have been decimated by breakage and loss — so included in that cupboard are plates that date back to the '70s, '80s and '90s — and if this is Grandma's kitchen, there are plates from the 1950's and earlier, too. Nobody worries that the plates don't match... nobody even notices anymore. In fact, everyone in the household has a favorite plate that they consider theirs. The same is true of the silverware, the glasses, and the cups.

Most fascinating to us, though, is the apparent unity of thought that has gone into stocking the kitchen tools... it is as if all the cooks got together and said, "I must have this... I don't need that..." Typically, here's what you'd find:

- Wooden spoons, stirrers, forks, all for handling sauces and soups and gravies.
- Good-quality ladle, usually stainless steel, because it gets a real workout.
- Several sizes and shapes of spatulas.
- Many pot holders, some homemade ones.
- Blender; not expensive — gets used a lot.
- Meat grinder, if livestock are raised.
- Food grinder, manual, if vegetables are canned — good for making relishes, purees, and other concoctions.
- Two or more frying pans. (The favorite is usually the old cast iron one.) Plus numerous pots and pans of various other sizes and shapes. Can't have too many pots.
- Dutch oven for baking beans and for cookouts.
- Canning pot, for "water-bath canning," a method of preserving some foods in a deep pot of boiling water, then removing and cooling the jars.
- Canning supplies such as lid-lifters, clamps, pouring funnel, mitts, and so forth; also several canning books.
- Canning jars — easily several dozen, with extra lids and bands.
- Pressure canner, alternatively used for pressure cooking tougher cuts of meat.
- Knives, many kinds, serrated edges and needle sharp, all in excellent condition.
- Mixing bowls, different sizes and shapes. The best are stainless steel, but you'll also see plastic ones.
- Egg beaters, usually an electric one AND a manual one.
- Manual can openers.
- Refrigerator, standard size... except at our house where two "mini" fridges hide beneath counters for extra space.

- Freezer. BIG freezer, and it's usually full.
- Stove — may be gas, electric, or wood/coal-fired — usually has a big oven (for the holiday turkey and baking several items at one time).
- Microwaves, because they have become so inexpensive, are also found now in many kitchens.
- Popcorn machine OR favorite old popcorn pan.
- Deep fryer, even though the health advocates in society say "fat is evil," people *still* love their deep fry.
- Toaster, two-slice size is typical.
- Bread pans, cake pans, angel food cake pans, bundt pans, jello molds, cookie pans, pizza pans, assorted sizes.

You usually won't find two specific items in a real country house: a dishwasher or a garbage disposal. The dishwasher isn't there because it's not a necessity... the kids get their practical experience in life by doing dishes, so it's not unusual to hear folks say, "Oh, I've got dishwashers — they're 12 and 15 (years old)."

Garbage disposals are a mess if you're on a septic system — the excess of food stuffs going directly into the tank can slow and gum up the works. Plus, why waste all those good leftovers, when you've got chickens, dogs, pigs...?

At its best, a real country kitchen is a working room, not only used for preparing meals, but also the place mom and pop relax with a cup of coffee while discussing plans. There's often a table and chairs or nook for meals in the kitchen — though not so often the fancy synthetic-topped items you see in the magazines. Sometimes, it's a plank table that someone is still planning to refinish one of these days; in other cases, it's Formica and shows its years... but it's clean.

Today, we give lip service to the idea that the kitchen is the "heart of the house," but in the country the kitchen serves as survival headquarters — pumping nutritious foods into the people, generating the scraps that will feed the livestock, organizing the food supply, making plans for next year, and providing a central location for all household activities.

These are not trivial activities... don't let anyone tell you otherwise.

Eating Country

There is a perception out in the waiting-to-be-country crowd that when you move to a farm, you are supposed to suddenly eat a healthy diet. That involves lots of whole grains, like wheat and rye, and certainly throwing in a bunch of vegetables you've never seen before in a supermarket, like rutabagas and arugula and casaba melons. Forget white sugar and white flour. These are sinful substances directly from Hell. On the surface, this is not necessarily bad advice.

BUT ...!

But before you take such statements as gospel, think of this: Changing your family's diet all at once will put considerable stress on everyone involved — on your family, because they will probably not go for this forced alteration in their eating habits, and on you, the fixer of the food, because your culinary efforts will be continually rejected.

❀

Nick: This ploy would not work in the city — should living in the country change things just because you read an article in some farm magazine that touted, to the heavens, the goodness of whole breads? So what! After fourteen years, I still don't care all that much for whole wheat bread (unless I'm really hungry). I'll eat a whole loaf of fresh baked white bread by myself, but my wife is pretty much the only one in our house that actually loves whole wheat loaves. And that's just the way it is.

ଓ

It is best to eat what you usually eat when you move to the country, adding different foods only when they meet with family approval. Foods you really enjoy, regardless of their health value may even help you through those stressful moments you will most likely encounter with your country move. These foods, of course, might include sugary desserts and the like. How about a nice big peach cobbler?

Try to get your psyche leaping with a big bowl of boiled wheat berries or a plate full of Swiss chard.

Living in the country doesn't have to mean culinary torture for you and your family. Want a full-scale mutiny? Then push this nonsense at the dinner table.

ଓ

CS

Chapter Six
All Creatures...

Livestock

*We used to look on farm animals with a kind of Old-MacDonald's-
Farm sentimentality, all the domesticated beasts living together,
and with humans, in gentle harmony, with a moo-moo here
and a cluck-cluck there.*

Livestock are not, generally speaking, pets. In spite of *All Creatures Great and Small*, you will find this to be true.

Hand-raised animals tend to be friendly enough (if you happen to find enough time to invest in hand-raising them), but, for the most part, farm creatures want to keep their distance, no matter how nice you are to them. They recognize instinctively that they are different from you, even if you don't.

As city people by birth, we used to look on farm animals with a kind of Old-MacDonald's-Farm sentimentality, all the domesticated beasts living together, and with humans, in gentle harmony, with a moo-moo here and cluck-cluck there. In reality, the family cow may spend most of her time in a state of gentle docility, and then, out of nowhere, kick you in the head. If you decide to keep chickens, you'll have a hard time keeping them out of your garden and eating your produce (and be warned, chickens are the worst cannibals you'll ever encounter this side of New Guinea). Ducks will poop up every standing-water container in sight. Geese will poop up everything. Your cats will eat baby chicks like popcorn. Horses are as hazardously unpredictable as delinquent children. Goats, the craftiest agents of Satan you will find in the animal world, will escape from wherever you put them, and eat whatever plants you value most. Sheep, the most pastoral of livestock in this book, will do their best to cure you of thoughts of their supposed passivity the first time you try to shear them or trim their hooves, by knocking you down, or kicking you somewhere tender.

Treat your livestock with respect, but don't expect them to be like humans. And don't trust them. Once you start thinking that they are reasonable and rational, they will remind you most painfully that you are certainly mistaken.

Believe it. We've had the bruises to prove it.

Doctoring Livestock

Livestock get sick. And unless you are in a position to always afford a vet, or you are a vet, you will doubtlessly have to learn something about treating animal ailments. Worming, vaccinating for various diseases, treating bloat and colic, setting broken bones, taking care of udders cut on barbed wire, hoof rot, founder, pink eye, mastitis, and fly strike, delivering babies alive and dead... you name it, you just might have to deal with it some time or another on your farm.

Be warned, however: Even when you can manage to cover those vet bills, livestock have a special way of falling ill during that record flood that cuts you off from the rest of the world, or whatever, where no one short of Santa in his flying sleigh can make it out to where you live.

Then, you'll be on your own — whether you like it or not.

You know, you can't just sit around and let an animal suffer or die because you're afraid to get your hands dirty, or you just don't know what to do. You have a responsibility when you keep livestock. Read. Call someone on the phone, and ask questions. That's how you learn.

We once had an old Morgan horse who came down with colic during one of the biggest snow storms we'd ever experienced in all our years on the farm. Colic, sometimes caused by an impacted bowel, is incredibly painful for a horse, and often leads to death. We consulted our veterinary book. It said to call a vet. Okay, we were in the middle of a near blizzard, and no vet was coming out to our farm, not with two feet of snow on the road. We thought and thought about what we might do. With a bit of knowledge about medicine, we ended up concocting a mixture of bran, molasses, and olive oil, which we hoped would get the horse's gut unclogged. We had a time forcing him to eat it; but we managed to get him to swallow enough of it. After that, to keep him from rolling around in pain on the ground, something that can cause a horse's intestines to twist, killing him for sure, we walked the old guy through the falling snow for the entire night. Next morning, both Nick and the horse were dragging, but, to put it as delicately as possible, the horse had a major bowel movement, which was just what we were looking for. That meant his obstruction was cleaned out. After that, he was fine. If we hadn't intervened with some kind of action, the horse would probably have died. But he was our horse, and our responsibility, so we did what we could for him.

If you have livestock, be ready to be your own vet. It'll happen.

Fences

Putting up good fences became a number one priority.
And when these were finally in place, I'd felt like
I'd been paroled from prison.

There is a saying: Good fences make for good neighbors. This is doubtlessly true; and yet, there is another important reason for having good fences. Without adequate fencing, you cannot control livestock. This is a simple fact. Chain link, barbed wire, wood slat, it doesn't matter. Animals on one side of a fence have to stay on that same side, if that is your intention. Otherwise, what you have is no good.

ᛣ

Nick: Our property was not adequately fenced when we first moved onto our farm in 1985; and, consequently, I was forever having to chase down our goats and sheep and horses, who decided 10 acres was not enough room for them to graze on. I used to blame them; but, of course, the responsibility was really mine.

I wasted hours and hours of my life hunting down my various creatures and herding them home, or chasing them off our neighbors' front lawn. They also sometimes got into our front yard and damaged our fruit trees. Physically, this situation was tiring; psychologically, it was stressful not knowing what those animals would try next. Of course, they always managed to do their worst when something important was going on. If we had to be somewhere at a specific time, they'd be sure to disappear to a place that would ensure we'd miss our appointment. You could almost count on that.

Eventually, it came down to actually doing the shepherding routine. Which was basically just standing there as a guard. Propped there on a hillside in the rain, or in a biting wind, shepherd's crook in hand, just to keep a pile of sheep and goats from wandering away. Talk about boring. Even worse, it kept me from doing something more productive with my time.

Putting up good fences became a number one priority. And, when these were finally in place — I had to build them myself — I felt like I'd been paroled from prison. Certainly, a huge weight, with a corresponding sense of impending doom, was lifted instantly from my shoulders. I knew if I went to town, where the livestock would be when I got home. I knew I was done with my animal hunts, hurrying frantically through the woods as darkness was descending over the countryside. It was wonderful.

 C3

If you can't manage farm animals, don't get any until you can.

Horse Farming

*The horse will not be impressed by your college education;
if you are going to work successfully with horses,
you have to understand them inside out.*

We've always liked the idea of using horses for farm work. It's so rustic, and there's a certain romance that goes along with horse farming. There are even certain advantages to using a horse rather than a tractor. Certainly, you don't have be a mechanic to keep a horse running smoothly. It won't run out of gas, or get a flat tire. And there's all that free fertilizer.

The mistake is in thinking that when you're living on a farm, you'll get yourself a couple draft horses or mules, or even regular everyday horses, or ponies, and just start plowing fields or hauling stuff around. We know people who are still in the hospital because they bought into that particular cute fantasy.

As colorful as horse farming is on paper, if you don't know what you're doing, you'll end up with broken bones or dislocated limbs. Horses in real life are not big, hoofed dogs. Keep this fact in mind when you have that picture of yourself plowing your field, like you were king of the Amish, or something. They are also not Black Beauty, or Flicka, or Zorro's horse. Don't confuse them with fiction. They can be friendly or cranky, as the mood hits them, and more changeable than you'd imagine. They can decide to hurt you, and there's nothing you can do about it. They don't even have to be mean to hurt you. They can hurt you when they like you. One chance fly bite on the rump of your equine can lead to a surprise kick that can leave you picking up your face in another time zone.

Having a higher IQ than the horse won't help you. Having a higher income than the horse won't help you. Being human won't help you. The horse will not be impressed by your college education. If you are going to work successfully with horses, you have to understand horses inside out. That's the only thing that will save you from serious injury, and even that is not always enough.

If using horses is a must for you, learn the ropes from someone who knows — not from a book, or worse yet, from just doing it.

The Calf Leaves Home:
A Tale of Civilization Versus Nature

Being city people, we had some pretty odd thoughts about how we were going to run our farm when we first moved to the Missouri Ozark Mountains.

One of our worst delusions dealt with how we were going to become cattle barons. We'd start with a single heifer calf, raise her up, have her bred, get a baby from her, and then we'd have a herd. Right?

That we knew nothing about cattle, had never owned livestock bigger than a rabbit, and were totally lacking in the necessary restraining areas — corrals, chutes, adequate fences, and whatnot — for the efficient management of creatures that had minds of their own (and huge bodies to back up their minds), didn't matter. That we were, perhaps, psychologically unsuited to cattle raising didn't matter. We were "smart" people from the city, and we'd make it work.

So, we went and bought ourselves a calf.

A black Angus heifer.

From the start, we kind of stumbled along, taking care of the animal in the blissful haphazard fashion of the totally ignorant. And in spite of us, she lived. And grew.

Six hundred pounds, and a few months later, we thought we were hot stuff. Cattle folks! Problems? Not one.

Then, one fine morning, out of the blue, the calf was gone.

It was as simple as that.

After a brief trek around our property and through the woods, there was no getting around it. She was nowhere to be found. Absent. Missing in action.

I was really mad. Lousy calf! Just when you start trusting livestock to act responsibly, they pull a fast one on you. Talk about ungrateful. We weren't even going to eat her.

"Where do you think she went?" Anita asked anxiously. "Do you think maybe... rustlers got her?"

"Gee, I don't know. I never thought about that."

Our neighbor, J.L. Kimbrough, had once told me that rustlers were still a big problem for cattlemen. These days, though, it was into a waiting livestock truck and a quick haul over the state line instead of the surreptitious cattle drive. J.L. added that when cattlemen caught rustlers before the sheriff did, well, it was mighty unpleasant for someone. He didn't elaborate on what might actually transpire during these impromptu get-togethers, but I was reasonably certain that I never wanted to be in the position of a captured cattle thief.

My wife peered uneasily out the kitchen window.

"Oh, don't be so paranoid," I said irritably.

"I'm not paranoid," she said. "I've read in the newspaper about cattle being stolen around here. Anyway, I can be paranoid if I want. I'm from Southern California."

"Well," I observed, "rustlers would have to be pretty desperate to swipe one lone calf. Besides, it's hard enough for us to catch her these days — and she knows us. Think how she'd take to being chased by someone she never saw before."

"But —"

"I'd bet twenty cents she just ran away."

"Where would she go?"

I thought for a moment.

"Could be she went over to visit Mr. Kimbrough's cattle."

"Do you really think so?"

"Well there's only one way to find out. I know where his herd is right now. I'll hike over and take a look. If she's there,

I won't have any trouble picking her out of the crowd. She's got warts."

"What will you do if you find her?"

I shrugged. "Oh, I don't know. Try to scare her home with stories of UFO cattle mutilations."

"Try again."

I hesitated as an idea formed in my head. "I — I don't know."

Anita narrowed her eyes. "Okay, what's going on that little head of yours?"

"What do you mean?" I asked, innocently.

"I recognize that tone. Every time you get that evasive catch in your voice. You end up doing something really dumb."

"No, I don't."

"Yes, you do."

"I don't."

"You do."

"Don't."

"Liar."

"You're the liar."

"So what are you going to do, dope?"

I smiled. "Maybe I'll just lasso the calf with a rope and drag her home."

"I knew it. You'll get yourself killed."

"No way. She's just a calf."

"A calf that weighs hundreds of pounds. How much do you weigh, skinny?"

"I'll dazzle that bovine with my footwork."

"Just don't bleed on her."

"Funny."

Anita shook her head. "All right, go ahead. Be a macho cowboy moron. See if I care."

"I know what I'm doing."

"Do you want that inscribed on your tombstone?"

"How about 'Nagged to Death'?"

Anita gave me an unexpected hug.

"What's that for?" I asked.

"You're a moron."

"You're hugging me because I'm a moron? That's different."

"Oh, shut up."

"Back to normal."

Anita looked worried. "You've made up your mind about this?"

I nodded. "Sometimes you just have to do stuff so you can look back and say you did it — even if you only did it once."

"I hate that."

"I'll be okay. I'm an adult. Besides, I know for a fact that God is keeping me alive so He can torture me."

"You are a moron," Anita said. "Go catch the calf."

Rope in hand, I headed off to track down J.L. Kimbrough's cattle. I also took along a can of corn to entice and distract our calf — if she was with them.

Amazingly, the herd was right where I thought it would be: in a large, open field about a mile from our farm. And, sure enough, the calf was with them. Black, scruffy and angular, with a perpetual glob of snot running down her snout, she was easy to spot.

I was right on two counts. I congratulated myself.

The rest, I reasoned, would be easy. I had the advantage — thousands of years of evolution on my side. It was a simple matter of brain over brawn. The calf didn't stand a chance, my city-bred brain told me. I'd simply throw a rope around her neck, and she'd give up, bowing to my obvious human superiority. No contest.

I really believed this. I grew up absorbing the Disney version of Nature.

I approached the animal very slowly.

"Hello, calf, calf, calf," I said softly. "You remember me, don't you?"

The other cattle scattered in a panic, but the calf stood her ground, staring at me with huge, damp brown eyes. I suppose she recognized me. She went back to eating grass, and swatting at flies with her tail.

"Calf," I said, shaking the grain can. "Look. I've got a nice snack for you. Yum, yum."

I inched my way toward her, and poured the food on the ground.

The calf took a cautious step forward, and buried her nose in the grain pile. She began munching contentedly.

"Okay," I whispered. "Stay right where you are."

I pulled on my leather work gloves, and got my rope ready to throw. Wrapping one end of it around my left hand, I dug my heels into the dirt.

While the calf was otherwise occupied, I took aim with the lasso, and let it fly. The loop fell neatly over her head. I pulled it tight.

"I've got you!" I shouted.

The calf shot upright in alarm. Startled, she bawled, and shook her head from side to side to throw off the offending line.

I tensed, ready for a struggle. I was confident I had the situation under control.

Then, the animal jerked back wildly, throwing her full weight and strength into the maneuver.

Before I knew what was happening, she yanked me off my feet as though gravity had been suspended. "Aagg!" I groaned, slamming to the ground like a sack of cement. Suddenly, I was bouncing across the field, arms and legs flailing. I tried to slow myself down, but it didn't do any good; the rope was firmly attached to my personage.

The calf, crying at the top of its lungs, ran madly across the clearing. Then, when she reached a fence, she turned around and ran back the other way. I hit every sticker bush, every rock, every small tree, every stump in sight. And it hurt. A lot. I didn't miss many cow pies either.

Evolution was coming in a poor second in this contest.

Finally, the calf stopped to rest. At this point, I was able to stagger to my feet. Blood was starting to soak through my clothing at various points of injury. I pulled a large thorn out of my right arm. Then, I undid the rope from around my aching left hand.

I had no idea what to do next.

It didn't matter, though.

All at once, the calf relaxed, and went back to eating grass. I couldn't believe it. I pulled slightly at the lasso, and she followed submissively. She'd given up. Why? Probably hauling me all over creation just wore her down.

"Let's go home," I said to her.

I'd taken about five steps when, without warning, something slammed into my butt. I flew through the air, giving what must have been a dazzling impression of a pinwheel, and landed a few feet away. Looking up from where I'd crashed, I saw an old Hereford cow glaring coldly at me. She must have thought I was hurting the calf, and decided to intervene with her head.

My own livestock, I noticed unhappily, was bounding away. The rope trailed behind her. Limping slightly, I took off after the creature.

I dove for the end of the tether, and missed. But luck was on my side. The calf charged through a thicket, tangling her leash in the branches of a large, sturdy bush. She pulled and pulled, but she couldn't free herself.

I hurried to where the escapee was trapped, intent upon recapturing her. Instead she abruptly circled around behind me. The taut rope, stretched between her and the plant, became a scythe, catching me right behind the legs. I flipped upside down, and landed on my head.

I laid on the ground for a long, long time before I was able to stand up again.

"I hate you, you stupid rat!" I yelled, as I staggered to my feet. I brushed myself off.

"You can stay there until you turn into hamburger, for all I care!"

I trudged off, grumbling to myself.

I was done with being a cowboy.

By the time I was half way home, I began feeling guilty about leaving the calf tied up. Once I calmed down, I realized I couldn't let her remain where she was. So, when I got back, I went over to J.L. Kimbrough's farm to enlist my neighbor's aid in dealing with the problem.

J.L., a cattleman for more than twenty-five years, listened to my story with amusement.

"It sounds," he said once I'd finished, "like you bit off a little more animal than you had teeth for."

I nodded, thinking, "Call me Mr. Gums!"

"Well, let's go see what we can do together," he suggested.

We drove in his truck back to where I'd left the calf. She was still there.

"So, what do you think?" I asked.

"Let's just let her loose," J.L. suggested. "She can stay with my cattle. She'll only run away again if we take her back to your place."

"You're sure it's no trouble?"

"I don't mind. There's plenty to eat in this field. One more animal won't make any difference."

"Okay," I agreed, "sounds good to me."

J.L. could have said, "Let's blow the bugger up with a stick of dynamite." I wouldn't have protested. I would have lit the fuse.

With the assurance of an accomplished livestock handler, Mr. Kimbrough calmed down the calf and slipped the rope from around her neck, at which point she shot off to join the other cattle.

"Don't you worry," he observed. "She'll be fine now."

Good riddance, I thought.

A month later, Anita and I traded the calf to J.L.'s son, Travis, for a 1967 Chevy Suburban. We were pleased with the deal. Our truck has never run away once.

This, needless to say, marked the end of our stint as cattle barons.

We bought some sheep! Little ones. Now, there was something we could manage. Sheep aren't any problem.

Want to bet?

Learning to Shear Sheep

I never do anything the easy way. At least, not until I'm covered with scars. For instance, what's the best way to get your sheep shearing done? Take a course? Hire someone who knows that he's doing? Good, reasonable ideas.

Forget it. Faced with shearing for the first time, I was able to get myself boxed into such a tight corner, there was no way the job could go smoothly. I was lucky my sheep didn't put out a contract on me after the ordeal was all over.

Talk about dopes. To start with, I waited too far into the season to get in touch with the shearer in our area. Well, what did I know? Suddenly, out of nowhere, it was the beginning of the summer, and there were twelve wool blankets hanging around the barnyard saying, "Excuse me, shouldn't we be naked now?" A friend, dropping by one day, added a cheerful note: "Don't those things die if you don't shear them?" Did they? Who knew? I sure didn't want to find out.

Have you ever sheared a sheep with a pair of scissors?
Not while you were sane, you say. Good response.

I felt doomed. Shepherding was fast losing its image of "easy" management. The fear of becoming an ex-shepherd hovered before me. I quickly came to the conclusion that something had to be done. Fast! Smart fellow!

"What now?" Anita asked. At the time, dropping cash into an electric shearing kit was out of the question.

"Do the job by hand?" I suggested.

"What are you planning to do — pluck them?"

"There is such a thing as hand shears, you know."

"Yes, but you may not have noticed we don't have any."

"You think I'm dumb? I know a neighbor who has a pair. His father-in-law used to shear sheep."

"When was that?"

"Around... around 1910."

"You're going to shear sheep with an antique. That's just wonderful."

"They're shears, that's what counts."

"No one uses hand sears anymore. It's hard enough shearing sheep with electric ones."

"It's better than having to give them all CPR when they get heat stroke."

My wife just smiled.

The hand shears were a disaster. In the years since they'd last been used on sheep, they'd been called into garden service, weeding, prying up rocks, pruning fruit trees and rose bushes, stuff like that. They'd also spent a number of years living outside. My neighbor handed them to me with the remark, "You know, my father-in-law always said the secret to these things was keeping them sharp."

"Are they sharp now?" I asked.

"They wouldn't cut paper. Do you know anything about sharpening tools?"

"No."

"There's a secret to sharpening hand shears."

"What's that?" I asked hopefully.

"I don't know."

"Ah. Well, I'll do my best with them."

He sighed.

"Take good care of those things. They're antique."

"I know," I said.

I tried to put an edge on the shears. I worked on them with a whet stone for two full hours. Then Anita and I caught a sheep to test them on. The wool just kind of mushed sadly between the blades.

"I guess they're not very sharp," I said.

"Looks like," she replied.

"I'll take them back."

"Good idea."

The sheep looked relieved that we'd apparently changed our minds about torturing it.

We went to a dozen hardware stores. No one had hand shears. "What the heck do you want hand shears for? Why don't you get some nice electric ones? Everyone uses electric these days," was the usual statement we ran into. "Thanks," we'd reply, nodding and smiling. Heads hanging we'd trudge back to our car. "What now?"

"Who knows?"

Have you ever sheared a sheep with a pair of scissors? Not while you were sane, you say. Good response. I probably wasn't quite mentally sound when I decided to go that route. But at least they were sharp.

"Do you know how you're going to do this?" Anita asked.

I'd been so busy thinking about finding something to shear with I hadn't actually given the rest of the job much thought.

"Well," I said slowly, "you sort of start at the head, and just kind of work your way downward. Don't you?"

"You'll do real well," she said. "Leave the ears and hooves on, please."

The very first sheep I trimmed took me four hours. It was, mildly put, an ordeal for all concerned. It was more of an inch by inch manicuring than it was shearing. That the animal survived is a testament to the innate hardiness of sheep.

The next woolly I encountered only took me two hours. I was definitely improving.

My worst moment came when a hefty ewe of about 170 pounds managed to throw me off balance with her squirming. She knocked me down, and danced an energetic flamenco on my chest while I held her around the neck. This went on for what seemed like hours until, losing her footing on my deflating body, the sheep rolled over onto its own back, and came to rest in the crook of my arm. At this point, it gave up its energetic protestations and just lay there calmly. She looked over at me, blinking innocently. I got the feeling she was saying, "So what do you say? I'm ready to get back to work if you are." I wasn't. (I still have a crook-neck squash-shaped scar on my back — my kids call it the "fossil" — from that wrestling match.)

Over a one month period, I eventually cut my shearing time down to around sixty minutes per sheep. Why did it take so long to trim only twelve sheep? Well, you don't speed through something you're having that much fun at, don't you know. You want to savor it, to make it last. If you believe that, I have a great pair of shearing scissors you might want to buy.

The following year, out of an unrelenting horror of my previous hand-oriented tribulations, Anita and I bought a brand new pair of electric shears. I also studied. I finally wised up some. But I never could spin the sheep the way they were supposed to go. "It's all in the way you use your feet!" I learned. My feet were obviously being controlled by space aliens. I knew where they were supposed to go, but they always ended up somewhere else — usually tipping the animal into the best positions for an escape.

Another thing: Whenever I watched the pro-shearer tackle his job, somehow his sheep always seemed different from my sheep. His cutters glided effortlessly over those bodies that were always and forever rigid and wrinkle-free. My sheep, on the other hand, seemed to melt when I touched them, and had deep, uncooperative folds in places I didn't even know they had skin. I felt like I was trimming jelly fish.

I did twenty-six sheep this time. Average shearing time — twenty minutes. A big improvement. For me. Hey, I never said I was good, did I?

Predators

Wild animals are not fun things. Coyotes will look on your farm as a personal grocery store if you let them. Skunks and possums go for chickens and eggs, hawks and owls will fly away with anything small that isn't nailed down. Snakes will eat all the eggs your chickens produce. Pet dogs, believe it or not, are the biggest decimators of sheep flocks in the United States.

You may want to live in harmony with Nature, but Nature may end up looking at your livestock as a free meal. You may start off being an eco-pacifist, refusing all forms of guns, but when that dirty old raccoon comes around and chews the heads off all your baby ducks, you may change your mind about firearms. If you just can't get past the gun phobia thing, bows and arrows work, and there's little chance of accidentally shooting yourself — unless you happen to be one of the Three Stooges. Baseball bats will do some major damage, too, if you can get close enough.

There are, of course, humane traps that you can catch weasels and the like in. But as long as your predator has food outside the cage, he won't have much use for your trap. But even if you catch your adversary, where do you let him loose? Few places, even in the country, are near nothing anymore. Your carnivorous parolee just becomes someone else's problem.

Remember this: Once a predator gets started, it usually won't stop until the lunch counter is empty. If you have farm animals, it's your responsibility to them to protect them. Predators rarely go away on their own.

Only Walt Disney's idyllic world has friendly animals that love each other. And even that's gotten a little iffy in the past decade or so.

Learning from Our Mistakes:
Thanksgiving

I've heard farmers talk about how livestock can sense weather changes, how they can sense the danger of unseen, lurking predators, how they can sense fear, how they can even sense earthquakes. Most of all, how they can sense when you have something really important you want to do. This, as almost everyone who raises animals will agree, is when they make sure to complicate matters.

Knowing this, I should have realized I was doomed the moment we decided to have our Thanksgiving dinner at my wife's sister's house.

Of course, it started innocently enough (like the first page of any really good horror novel). "Why don't you go bring the sheep into the barnyard now?" Anita said to me, "We'll be leaving soon."

Until we finally got our back acreage fenced in properly, we always brought our sheep up to the barnyard when we left the farm for extended periods. It kept them out of mischief while we were absent — finding spots in our neighbor's fence line to sneak through (our Jacobs especially liked to treat fences as though they weren't there), getting into the front yard and eating all the bark off our fruit trees, fun stuff of that sort. With dogs chained strategically around the barnyard, it also acted as a form of predator control (the barking of countless well-placed canines has been instrumental in our record of never losing a single animal to coyotes in five years of farming).

"It won't take long," I replied, off-handedly. "I think I'll get dressed up first."

"Are you sure you want to do that?"

"Why not?"

"What if you get dirty? You know we're supposed to be over at my sister's at 5:30."

"I know that."

"Well —"

"Come on. What's so difficult about bringing up the sheep? I just saw them out by the pond. It'll take me ten minutes tops to get them put away."

"When did you last see them?"

"Oh, maybe half an hour ago."

Anita shrugged.

"If you say so."

The sheep were not at the pond. Surprise!

I shouldn't have been surprised. But I was. Maybe with the approach of the upcoming holidays, I'd deluded myself into thinking that the animals would magically evolve into considerate, helpful, reliable entities, transformed by the enchantment of the season. It worked for Ebenezer Scrooge. But the sheep must have missed that particular story.

I shook my head.

"Where'd those rats go?" I noticed my teeth were starting to clench.

I scanned our field. It was lamentably devoid of ruminants. Unless, I thought, grasping momentarily at a desperation-induced straw, unless they were lying flat on their stomachs in the tall grass, just to tease me, to pay me back for all those shearings and wormings. A quick trot over in the direction of a potential hiding place revealed the obvious; the sheep were not there. It was as though they'd been sucked into the fourth dimension.

I sighed.

Painful as it was, I had to face facts.

I knew I had to go and look for them. Now, I'd showered, I was wearing my best clothes, my boots were shined. I was ready for dinner — images of roast turkey, sweet potatoes, mashed potatoes, green peas, cranberry sauce, pumpkin pie, the works, filled my brain — not heading up a one-man search party. But I didn't have time to go back to the house and change. I'd have to go out "as is."

I ran to the other end of our field, hoping against hope that the sheep were nearby.

Nothing.

Finally, I found myself standing at the edge of the woods at the back of our property. My spirits plunged. I knew, beyond a shadow of a doubt, that the sheep were in there. Somewhere. My life was over. Forty acres of trees, rocks, bushes, vines, and steep hillsides stretched before me.

Of course.

To makes matters worse, it was getting dark. Very quickly.

I rushed headlong into the looming tangle. Newly-naked tree branches waiting for winter's breath swatted me sharply in the face, grabbed at my shirt sleeves, and knocked off my cap. I plunged on. I didn't have time to be careful. To say I was nervous makes me sound too calm. I was spending more time wiping old spider webs out of my eyes than I was looking for my sheep.

I was getting nowhere.

My lungs laboring, I collapsed on a rotting stump. I realized I had to put some reason into the hunt, or I'd never find anything.

I began criss-crossing the woods, focusing my explorations into defined areas. If anything would flush out the fugitives, this was it.

I was making pretty good time, too, that is, until I tripped at the top of an incline and tumbled head-long, bouncing and skidding, to the bottom of a gully. I landed, arms and legs outstretched, in a crunchy brown carpet of oak leaves, which would have been comfortable except for the sharp rock gouging me impolitely in the back.

I didn't care. I lay there covered in dirt and rotting plant life, groaning loudly. Why not? No one could hear me. I might as well enjoy myself in between the pain and thinking what a goof I was. I toyed with the idea of early retirement.

I'd almost convinced myself that I was too old for this kind of nonsense when a faint sound came to my ears. I recognized it immediately. *Bahhhhh! Bahhhhh! Bahhhhh!* Sheep! They were somewhere in the vicinity.

I struggled to my feet, and strained my ears to zero in on which direction they were coming from. It seemed like they were coming from my left.

I set off at a slow hobble. Up one hill, and down the other side. I stopped to listen.

Suddenly, there they were, above me on the next incline.

"Hey, you sheep!" I called out.

The animals, hunting nonchalantly amid the forest growth for acorns, raised their woolly heads en masse, saw who was attempting to interfere with their evening snack, and then went back about the business, an unspoken "forget that geek" if there ever was one.

I picked up a stick, and made my way around behind the escapees to start driving them. We were maybe a quarter of a mile from home. It would be completely dark by the time we got back.

I came to an abrupt halt. There, amid the foragers, was a ewe with a brand new lamb, so new it was still covered with the birth sack, orangy, wet, and steaming in the cooling night air.

It was pretty yucked up, but there was no time to be particular. Without hesitation, I scooped up the baby in my arms, and started the trail drive.

"Go home, sheep!" I yelled.

The sheep began moving. I followed. To be on the safe side, I took one last look behind me, just in case I'd missed anyone. There was the new mother turning back, looking desperately for her lamb. I hurried behind her, heading her off, and held the baby in front of her face.

"Look, look, here it is!" I said to the sheep.

The small form in my hands called to its mother. The ewe answered. I started off, holding the lamb where the ewe could see it. Head stretched forward, she followed.

At the same time, I had to prod the rest of the herd into motion again. Every time I took my attention off them, they spread out and went back to eating.

To complicate matters, occasionally, the mom would lose sight of her lamb in the dark, and turn back at a steady trot for the spot where she'd given birth. I'd have to cut behind her and thrust her offspring back into view. "Here's your baby. Remember? Pay attention!" Then, we'd be okay for another 50 feet or so.

The lamb wriggled and twisted to get out of the grasp of the monster that held it fast. Understandably, it wanted its mother. It kicked and threw its head from side to side. With every movement, I felt bits of damp, mucousy birth sack splatter in my face and hair. It went all over my shirt and pants, too, sticking firmly and soaking in. I was covered from head to foot. If there was any hope my appearance had survived the plunge down the hillside, all chances for acceptable neatness were dashed to bits in a hail of clammy goop. I was ready for dinner with zombies, but that was about it.

Anita was waiting at the barnyard gate when the sheep and I came rolling out of the darkness.

"Where were...?" she began impatiently. Then she saw the lamb in my arms. "I'll get a pen ready," she said, without missing a beat. She rushed into the barn.

"Are we late for dinner?" I called after her.

Anita's reply was instantaneous.

"You've got to be kidding."

Death

Here, we're speaking about animals, not you.

A fact of farm life: Livestock become deadstock.

Be ready for this one. For some people who've never raised livestock before, and think of animals as furry humans, this can be very traumatic. We can recall when we lived in the city, we almost never saw anything dead.

Not just the fact that you've lost a pet — or worse, a friend — but there's the problem, with the really, really big ones, of disposal. Chickens, rabbits, ducks — small things are easy to lose. If nothing else, they can be dumped in a quickly dug hole and covered over, or trotted off for a pitch in the woods.

On the other hand, we know some folks who, when their chicken flock was slaughtered by a neighboring farmer's dog, took what was left of their deceased fowl, cleaned them up a bit, and popped them into the freezer for later dinners. This was a bit much, to our way of thinking. They also make use of road kills. They actually travel around with a shovel and plastic bags in their truck.

Yet what do you do with a really big animal that decides to take a dirt nap? Anyone who moves to the country and buys a horse or cow doesn't start off picturing it belly up next to the kitchen door. But to ignore the possibility of it happening is asking for problems.

In days gone by, there was someone called a knacker who came out to farms when something large died, cutting it up and carting off the chunks. The carcasses were later turned into animal food and fertilizer.

Today, there might be professional knackers around, but don't count on it. A friend of ours who farms with two gigantic draft horses once said to us, "Gee, I don't really know what I'd do if one of these big guys dropped dead in my barnyard." Cut them up yourself, maybe? Good luck. Hope your chainsaw blade is sharp. Yuck!

So, what do you do?

☙

Nick: Like a dope, I once tried burying a horse. He was very old, and he just plain fell over dead one night out in our field. Digging the grave took me eight straight hours of digging with a shovel, and even at that it wasn't a very good job. Worse still, the dogs kept uncovering him. Eventually, we found his skull on our front lawn! Just so I'd know what to do in the future, I asked my neighbor, who'd been a cattleman, what he did when one of his animals died. "I just hook them up to the tractor, and drag them out to the back forty. The coyotes, bugs, and buzzards do the rest."

Oh, you mean they don't have to go to the funeral home? Wow! Practical versus sentimental. Keep this in mind: They start to smell extremely bad after a few hours, especially in the summer.

I have a spot on our farm picked out where I'd like to be buried when I die. My only instructions to my wife are, "Bury me deep." I don't want the dogs digging me up and dragging me back up onto the front lawn. What an embarrassment that would be.

Remember: Animals do not live forever. Be ready for it. The small ones and the large ones.

☯

Chapter Seven
Systems, Dominos,
and One-Cow Economics

We live in strange times. On one hand, our "official" version of reality (provided by media and spin-meisters) is a glowingly healthy economy, an endlessly rising stock market, and jobs for all. On the other hand, a neighbor just got laid off work, an uninsured friend opens the bill for a three-day hospital stay and finds it will cost her more than the value of her home, and the local bank refuses to believe you made that deposit — even though you've got the receipt. What gives?

All we have here are two different, and opposing, views of the same picture: One that is rosy, the other that is based on day-to-day reality. Which is more real?

It depends.

Depends on what you're looking for, and looking at. If you're the lady with the staggering bill in her hands, you fully understand that all the stock market hype in the world isn't a bit useful to you. If you're the guy with the bouncing checks, your bank's assurances of Y2K-compliance are pretty worthless.

That's because... the world-according-to-spin is happening outside of your real-world, true-to-life "system."

Country life is a system unto itself. After a while, you begin to see the connections. Pretty soon, you wonder why the obvious is so hidden to most people. It's not so much that the "obvious is hidden" — it's just that most people never look for it, and so they can never see it.

In country living, you become aware of the dominos, the system built upon system upon system. For instance, you can't raise chickens in isolation — the grain that feeds them comes from somewhere (needed: a field, fertilizer, tilling equipment, seed source, harvesting equipment, storage facility), the water that gives them drink didn't just appear (needed: well or catchment system, pump, holding tank, purification system, piping); and the light bulb that warms the chicks was made someplace (needed: glass, refined metals, shipping, manufacturing plants, truckers, highways, supermarkets to sell bulbs, electricity generating plants, power lines, utility companies, fuse boxes).

Nothing on a country place is in isolation — everything becomes part of a circle of dependencies and interdependencies, a chain of dominos that extends back in time to the first guy to use a plow. But the most successful small farm operators have one critical factor in common: They keep as much of their dependencies *on farm*, as possible. They try to make their operation as self-sufficient as can be.

Now, clearly, this doesn't mean mining and smelting and blacksmithing metal every time you want a nail. But it can start small ...start with great practicality ...start in a way familiar to all our rural ancestors ...with a cow.

The one-cow farm meets derision from professional dairymen, from conventional ag-economists, and from people who dislike hard labor. No doubt about it: You won't get rich with a lone milk cow. You won't be able to collect dairy subsidies from the federal government. You won't even be able to take a spur-of-the-moment vacation.

But your average, nonfancy jersey-type cow will give you three or more gallons of fresh, creamy milk every day. With retail supermarket milk running about $2.37 per gallon, that's about $7 worth of "income" daily; about $50 weekly; $200 per month. Figure $2,000 annually, roughly 900 gallons of milk, for a ten-month lactation (period of milking).

Obviously, this isn't a cash income. And to the uninitiated, three or more gallons of milk a day seem like an awful lot. (How much can one person or family drink, anyway?) Besides, the commercial dairy operator rakes in only about 70 cents per gallon, which drops the cash value of the milk, wholesale, to approximately $600.

But the important point here isn't how much the milk is worth if its sold — it's what can be done with all that white gold within the on-farm system.

Properly handled and cared for, that one cow with her daily three gallons can produce every type of cow's milk cheese under the sun; can give enough butter, cream, sour cream, and ice cream to statiate any family; can provide 450 pounds of meat (her calf) for the table; can increase the household egg supply; can help raise and fatten a couple of hogs (which further contribute meat, cooking lard, and soap); and can provide more than enough manure to heavily fertilize the garden. Dominos in action.

Let's look at some figures to determine whether this one little cow is worth her keep and your effort.

Cost of one dairy cow, milking: $500

Expense to keep: An acre of decent pasture, presumed already owned or rented; 20 pounds of 16 percent grain ration daily (more or less, depending on size — small jerseys can get by on five pounds daily) at about 10 cents per pound, roughly

$700 per year; at least one ton of good hay annually, depending on type and quality of pasture, about $120.

Breeding fee: $25 if artificially inseminated; or may be able to barter for a neighbor's bull's services.

Incidental costs: Vet bills, if any (annual TB and brucellosis tests are recommended); access to some sort of shelter during inclement weather.

Total purchase and maintenance, first year: About $1350 to $1450.

So, even including the cost of buying the cow, she still should produce enough retail-value milk, $2,000 worth, the first year to offset her purchase and keep.

The second year, maintenance should run only about $845, and that's if all feed and other services are purchased. If our farmer grows even a modicum of feeds (a stand of corn, some pumpkins, a quarter-acre of wheat or alfalfa), then expenses are considerably reduced.

Besides, so far we've been considering only the value of whole milk. Cheese — real, homemade "farmhouse" cheese — is now the province of gourmet stores; too expensive even for supermarkets! A typical "farmhouse" cheddar runs around $5 per pound or higher, while mass-produced grocery-store cheeses are closer to $3. A gallon of milk, skimmed of its cream, yields about a pound of farmhouse cheese, with a supermarket value of $3, and probably the only item required to make it that isn't already in most kitchens is a rennet tablet (actually, just a fourth of a tablet).

Each gallon of hand-skimmed milk also provides about a quart of cream, which can easily be turned into a half-pound or more of butter, worth about $1 in the supermarket.

Consequently, in terms of cheese and butter, an average cow's daily output is more like $12 to $18 retail — 3 pounds of cheese and 1½ pounds of butter. If a family drinks 3 gallons of milk a week, they could still produce an additional 18 pounds of cheese and 9 pounds of butter!!! And, of course, some of the cream can also be used to make ice cream, cream cheese and sour cream.

The bonus to this phenomenal food production is the cheese and butter-making leftovers: whey and buttermilk. Both of these are nutritious liquids, suitable (and then some!) for human consumption. Traditionally, however, this is the stuff of outstanding eggs and meaty hogs. Three pounds of cheese give back around 2 gallons of whey; butter returns about 2 cups per quart of cream used.

In feeding hogs, a pound of whey is roughly the same nutritionally as a pound of grain, so the leftovers from one day's cheese production can give a porker the equivalent of 8 pounds of feed! Free-ranging chickens, too, will come running when the whey bucket appears.

And then, there is the annual calf.

At birth, a calf weighs around 100 pounds. By the time it's three months old it should tip the scales at some 300 pounds. If the calf is a steer and is left to grow for nine months to a year, it'll provide more than 450 pounds of quality meat for the table. There are, of course, additional costs in raising a calf, but the feed bills can be offset by keeping it with its mama on good pasture. But doesn't that mean no milk for the farmer?

Not necessarily. In a plan formulated by "contrarian farmer" Gene Logsdon, the calf is kept full-time with the cow for the first two weeks of its life, then separated either during the night or during the daytime. After the twelve hours that the cow and calf are kept apart, the milk can be collected for the farmer's use: about 2 gallons worth. Then, the cow and calf are allowed to spend the rest of the day together. In this way, the baby benefits by receiving a normal feeding and bonding experience, and the farmer still gets his milk! An advantage to this is that the farmer has to milk only once a day and can even skip a milking or two if the cow and calf are kept together all day.

Ultimately, what happens when you own a cow is more than just a sudden urge to create mountains of specialty cheese and butter — it is a movement of country life into a system, into a pattern of dominos that goes far beyond that one cow.

It becomes almost a necessity to acquire a hog or two to take care of the extra milk production. The chickens will lay more consistently, and their eggs will taste better. Chicks grow faster and stronger on that whey. And, naturally you'll want to expand your garden spot, since the straw and manure quickly overwhelm a small plot. Then garden production dramatically increases, and soon you'll be storing and preserving the extra food.

That one dairy cow not only provides milk and meat economically, but also gives valuable lessons in cooking, preserving, bartering, gardening, and animal husbandry. She can help put families back on the sure road to self-sufficiency.

(The same, incidentally, could be said about three or four dairy goats — giving 3+ gallons of milk daily — with one important security added: if your one cow dies, your domino system is in deep trouble — but if one of four goats dies, you just cut back a little!)

What we have just walked through here is a critical thought process that can make or break your country life. Too often, educated and talented people with urban skills *assume* that country living lacks complexity — that because they understand physics or computer science or accounting, then raising a dumb ol' sheep ought to be really easy.

But you cannot raise "a dumb ol' sheep" — you can only incorporate that critter into a *system* that consists of your country place and the world around it.

Before you plunk down the cold, hard, cash for those new dominos ...think. Think hard. Figure out all the threads and strands of connections. Solve the problems before they even come into existence.

You'll spare yourself a lot of grief.

Your Farm as a Business Venture

At one time, we had a flock of more than seventy sheep.
We sold lambs, wool, meat, and breeding animals.
We started with commercial white-faced sheep
and ended up with exotics.

There'll come a time when you look around at those acres surrounding your home, and you'll say to yourself, *Maybe I could put this land to use.* At first, you may decide to use it to grow some crops for you and your family: corn, tomatoes, potatoes, strawberries, peppers, whatever. Or perhaps you'll want to have a few productive farm animals, such as cows, goats, chickens, or rabbits, to supply you with some of those basics: meat, eggs, milk.

But, then, perhaps you want to be more than a subsistence farmer with your farm. Perhaps you want to make money using your property. This can be done, but, more often than not, it has to be done in an intensive way — a heck of a lot of work and cash.

Unfortunately, if you are new to your area, a business venture concerning your farm often must take quite a bit of preparation. You have to make connections with the locals, establish a rapport, develop a market for what you want to sell and then advertise. Even then, you run the risk of falling flat on your face.

For one thing, is your area right for what you want to offer it? We recall reading about a farmer who developed a huge market for young goats in his part of the country. The article went on and on about his hard work, and his business sense; but, by reading between the lines, we got the real story. This guy lived near a big city that had a huge ethnic population that needed young goats for certain religious ceremonies two or three times a year. That was his primary, almost entire, market. Without that specific group, he would have had no business. Consequently, minus a huge goat-consuming ethnic group in your area — let's say you live somewhere in the vicinity of Muddy Gap, Wyoming, — investing a ton of cash in a pile of goats might be a major mistake on your part.

Moreover, is your area ready for what you want to offer? New ideas aren't necessarily wrong. They may just need time to take root and grow. This means that sometimes being able to stay in for the long haul is the only way to make your farm business a reality. That can be tough to do, of course, if the cash runs low or out. You have to live. You have to pay your bills.

Do you want to sell a crop? Sometimes nearby towns will have farmer's markets. Most of the ones we've seen, though, seem to be small time, supplemental income efforts, not major lifetime businesses.

Once or twice, over the years, we've known individuals who managed to set up pretty good businesses on their farms. One lady had a money-making rabbitry. She had more than 200 bunnies producing babies, and she sold to a buyer in another state. It was a full time job. She spent all her day cleaning cages, feeding and watering, and breeding and rebreeding her does. She actually made a living doing this for a number of years — until her buyer declared bankruptcy. Then, she had no one to sell her rabbits to.

There used to be big money in raising exotic livestock: llamas, ostriches and emus, rare breeds of sheep, goats, pigs; even hedgehogs. There was once a huge amount of money to be made in this field. It was a very much inflated field, though, a kind of pyramid scheme, where breeders were pretty much selling to potential breeders who would later sell to other potential breeders, and so on.

Truthfully, selling to other breeders was really the only market for exotics. If you bought an ostrich for $25,000, for instance, you weren't about to eat it for your Christmas dinner. You needed somebody to buy your ostrich eggs at $5,000 a pop. All this was a huge deal in the 1980s and early 1990s. We don't know how much of this stuff still goes on today. If it does, we'd be very careful of it. Last we heard, ostrich eggs were selling for a measly $25 each — talk about a market crash!

Investing in livestock you know nothing about can be very risky. We had a friend who mortgaged his farm for $50,000, and bought a pile of calves he hoped to raise and sell, multiplying his investment many times over. Every calf he bought died, and he lost his farm. He also lost his family, tried to commit suicide, and ended up in a state mental institution for a while. We don't know where our friend is living now.

But even if you do know your livestock inside out, you aren't necessarily any better off. We raised sheep for many years. At one time, we had a flock of more than seventy animals. We sold lambs as pets. We sold sheep for food. We sold breeding animals. We started with commercial, white-face sheep, and ended up with exotics. We raised four-horned, black-spotted Jacob sheep, which are a very old and rare breed. We worked hard at what we did. We also sold the wool we shared from our animals to spinners and weavers.

After twelve years, we probably broke a little less than even on the proposition. There was no real market for our sheep's wool. Sheep just aren't a big deal in the United States. Eventually, our flock became little more than pets, something we didn't especially need. They consumed a huge amount of hay and grain, diverting a significant amount of our overall income from other enterprises. We finally sold most of our flock to some folks who just wanted to have a pile of neat sheep, which is what our flock certainly was. We have only a few sheep now to help keep our fields from becoming overgrown. That is their job. Our sheep business is finished.

Don't be discouraged, however. It's important to know all these kinds of things, certainly before you invest your time, money, and your life, into something that may become a whirlpool, sucking you down into a financial morass. If you're going to turn your farm into a successful business venture, know as much as you can about the proposition you're thinking of investing in. Of course, nothing is completely safe. Even with the best planning in the world, you will be faced with risks. But, by dealing with your enterprise honestly and sensibly, at least you can minimize your chances of failure.

Be cautious investing in exotic animals, such as llamas.
What's trendy today could be worthless tomorrow.

Finally, don't be greedy. Don't invest everything you own, if you can help it. If your business possibility seems too good to be true, it probably is.

Job Opportunities

Unless you plan on plugging into a full-time 9 to 5 occupation in the nearest town to keep your country situation secure, be ready to pounce on a variety of part-time jobs whenever, and wherever, they pop up. They may not be secure in terms of fringe benefits and a steady, reliable paycheck, but they won't tie you down and detour you from developing your country dream.

Over the years, we have worked, together and separately, in the following capacities: secretary, magazine advertising manager, gourmet food store clerk, house painter, arts society coordinator, shepherd, fund-raiser, dog kennel cleaner, free-lance writer, photographer, fence builder, artist, magazine editor, gardener, hired hand, computer programmer, rabbit raiser, hay hauler, housesitter, sheep-hoof trimmer, sign painter, newsletter publisher, fencing master, free-lance antique salesperson, fruit picker, election worker, yarn store owner, book seller, video production. The list goes on and on.

If nothing else, it makes for an interesting life.

Of course, you may want to go the route of trying to make your farm pay for itself one hundred percent. And that certainly seems like an obvious way to go, doesn't it? But, you know, it's almost impossible to do this unless you start by buying into an already working operation of some sort. Setting up buyers and markets for what you have to sell can take years when you start from scratch. There are exceptions to this, and they do get written about in various farm-oriented publications; but that's because they are unusual. Remember that. No one writes about the everyday, common stuff of the farm work. The pitfall of these success stories is that they hinge on one or two particular details that are appropriate to that business only: location to some specific market or whatever. What might work well outside Atlanta, Georgia, may have absolutely no chance of succeeding outside Boise, Idaho. It's almost never clear-cut that anyone can do this thing. You have to use your judgement when you read this stuff.

A rule of thumb: stick with what you know. If a voice tells you to build it and they will come, check yourself into a local hospital fast. That was only a movie.

Ups and Downs, Ins and Outs, of Auctions

Before we moved to the country, we heard about "those great farm auctions" — where (it was said) you could get incredible bargains on all kinds of animals, tools, equipment, and household goods.

Today, after fifteen years of practical experience — it ain't what it seems. Oh, sure... there are bargains, really good bargains. But... there's also an awful lot of ways you can end up with unbelievable junk that cost a fabulous sum. Even more confusing, buying at auction is considerably different than selling at auction.

How do you navigate the system? Here are some tips:

1. There are two kinds of auctions: on-farm and at an auction house. The on-farm variety is generally the product of a farmer going out of business, or a financially-strapped farmer selling "extras" to meet some bills, or an estate being liquidated (i.e., the city grandkids sell all of grandpa's old farming stuff). The auctioneer comes directly to the farm, where all the goods and livestock are looked over or sorted through. Usually, portable signs will mark the way and identify the place where the auction is being held — and there will be lots of potential buyers' cars and trucks parked around. The auctioneer walks among the goods, and the crowd of buyers follow along.

The auction-house version is generally "item" sales — a couple of goats or sheep, or exotic livestock, or a bull, or a pony, or whatever. Here, the seller takes his "items" to the large auction house, and the goods are put on display. If the seller has livestock, there are pens and handling chutes that move the animals through a maze right up to the selling booth. The booth is either a platform and podium (for selling goods), or a pen (for livestock). The items or animals are brought individually or in a small group right in front of the seated crowd, so buyers can bid to their heart's content without even having to stand up.

2. There is a charge to sellers to use the services of an auctioneer, whether they make a profit or not. This can vary between 15-25% of the selling price of the item or animal — or may be a fixed price per head ($10 for cattle, $3 per head for sheep or goats, for example). As a seller, if the prices your livestock goes for is poor, you may actually end up owing the auctioneer and have *minus* profit. Yes, we *have* seen sheep sell for $2 per head — which means the poor seller had to fork over $1 per sheep for the privilege of running them through the auction house.

3. Auctioneers are charming, likeable guys (or gals). They are humorous, entertaining, and plain fun to watch. They also have an veracity level that makes a politician look like the Pope.

To be fair, no auctioneer can possibly know all the details about any one item or animal — they see thousands and thousands of sale goods every week, and can't be expected to know what they're looking at every time. We watched a trio of beautiful, full-coated cashmere goats be described as "straight hair angoras" — and sold for $23 per head ...this was when cashmere goats were selling in the thousands of dollars. Friends bought a Bashkir curly horse, an even tempered rare breed noted for its poodle-like hair, for $200 — the auctioneer said it was a "mule." An auctioneer looked under the tail of a fluffy black sheep and pronounced it an "ewe" — while the animal was urinating from mid-belly. We sold a large-size two-horned Jacob sheep ram, with a heavy wool coat and gorgeous spotting that the auctioneer called a "Barbados" ram (a brown hairsheep) — no one could hear our anguished cries from the far back of the bleachers!

The shyster auctioneer isn't just a legend. We've watched auctioneers make deals with their friends *right in front of the sale crowds* and overheard them offer to start selling "low" so their friends could buy easily. It wouldn't be impossible for an auctioneer to purposefully mislabel some item or animal to make sure the crowd doesn't know what's really being offered (we still wonder about those cashmere goats....).

The question here is, "How much can you believe about what an auctioneer says?" The answer: *Only what you can confirm with your own eyes!*

However, here's a caveat to that: *Even if it looks good, assume it isn't!* Livestock, machinery, water and air-tight stuff, equipment of all kinds, autos and trucks....just because they look okay, doesn't mean they are. Start and run all vehicles, inspect doors, windows, locks, lights, moving parts, tires, oil level — anything that could affect the safety or use of the device. Anything that is supposed to hold liquids, sniff the interior — you don't know what was last in there otherwise. Milking machines need to be tested — maybe the inflation is bad in one, maybe it hasn't been cleaned in a couple of months. Look for signs of rust on anything advertised as "stainless steel" — if there's rust, it isn't.

Livestock, especially, need to be very closely checked, and even then, you'll be happier in the long run if you assume the animals aren't going to make you any money. Example: a friend took her vasectomized teaser ram to auction. He was a big, meaty, crossbred animal — must have weighed more than

300 pounds. She told the gate keeper the animal was a "teaser" — but the auctioneer announced the sheep was a "pleaser ram" (whatever that means). Pity the poor unsuspecting buyer whose ewes all were barren the next year.

Another one: A lady had a cow that suffered serious complications during calving. The vet thought it should be put down, but the lady stitched the cow herself, filled it with antibiotics, and waited. The cow got better, but was sterile afterwards. At auction, the cow was to have been sold to the meat market, but sold instead to a cow/calf operation....

More: A Nubian doe waiting to be sold, abruptly kids a small single. The auctioneer scoops up the still-wet baby and auctions it for $15 dollars — the anxious doe follows, and is sold to a different buyer. How long before that baby gets its first much-needed colostrum? How many (and what kind) of bacteria was it exposed to immediately after birth? What kind of ancestry did it have? Did the doe deliver the placenta? Too many questions and too few answers...

4. If you want to bid (buy), you will need to sign up or register with the auction representatives before the auction. You may be expected to demonstrate your method of payment (i.e., show your checkbook, or riffle your cash). Auctions in my area *do not* accept credit cards or ATM cards — and cash is definitely preferred. Be prepared — bring more than you think you will need!

After signing up, you'll receive a card with a number, and that will be your "bidding number." In some auctions, you'll be expected to hold this up or wave it to show you are bidding — in others, you just shout your number when they ask who you are... each little auction has its own etiquette.

5. A word about "auction fever": DON'T!!! Auction fever is the act of bidding against another person for an item you want

long past the value of the item. It's basically a desire to "do better" than the other guy — to get the item at any price.

Auctioneers *love* bidders with auction fever, and they will feed your ego, goad you on, and try to get the bidding faster and higher.

One of the first auctions we attended had a pony with a single-seat (hackamore-type) cart and tack, to sell as a set. Before we laid eyes on the rig, the auctioneer's helper told us several families had come for the pony set, that the pony was young, healthy and very good tempered — ideal for little kids like the two we were dragging along. The cart was in "excellent" condition, just needed a little "fine tuning", and the kids would have the time of their lives...

Upon closer inspection, well, the pony's teeth indicated he was upwards of 20 years old. His feet were as flat as pancakes from years of foundering. His disposition was *really* calm — that kind of distant, empty, calm that animals get just before they keel over. The cart was 75 percent rust; both tires were flat. It looked as though it had been rammed by a truck. The tack was leather, brittle, and torn in several places. We decided not to bid.

Imagine our disbelief when the three other families decided they just *had* to have the set. Bidding started at $300. The parents rapidly bid, kids hanging on coat sleeves — pretty soon, angry shouted numbers rang out, faster and faster, up $25, up $35... up, up, up... we couldn't take it after the price reached $825. I had to walk away... this was at a time when a brand shiny new pony cart went for $300, and normal ponies could be easily found for $150.

Bidding stopped, we found out later, at $1,100.

The auctioneer was happy; the seller was ecstatic. The buyer got junk. Very expensive junk. At least the pony was going somewhere he could die in peace.

Similar auction fever can be expected among items that are considered "collectible" — spinning wheels, fancy cast-iron wood cook stoves, old plates, dolls, looms and so forth.

6. *Real* bargains are possible. But only if you are absolutely sure of what you are buying, and of what the going price for these items are. One man, who was shopping for cattle, found a plain porcelain wood cook stove, rusty but otherwise useable, at a farm sale. While he'd been looking for a wood-fired cooker, he had found that new stove prices were exorbitant. He waited after the cattle were sold, hung around the length of the hot afternoon, and stood by to see what the stove went for. The auctioneer called for bids — silence from the small crowd. "Who'll give me $10?" he said. Silence. "$5?" Silence. Our man bid $3 — and took home the stove that has been heating his house in winter and cooking most of their meals for the past three years.

☙

Anita: My brother had priced new cisterns (water holding tanks). He found that plastic cisterns ran about $1 per gallon — so a 350 gallon tank cost about $350. He decided to go to a farm sale that advertised two bulk milk tanks. Both tanks were stainless steel, in excellent clean condition, and held 800+ gallons each. One sold for $150; the other went to my brother for $120 — cost an extra $100 to move and settle it. It won't wear out for his entire lifetime, and ended up costing less than a plastic tank half its size. Plus, it had an electric cooler attached, so my brother can keep his summer water frosty. That's a bargain!

☙

Another case: At a livestock auction, a pod of five yearling ewes were sent into the selling pen. We recognized their ear tags as belonging to a regional producer of top-quality Polypays, a breed noted for multiple births. The ewes were recently shorn, looked to be in good breeding condition, and sold (but not to us!) for $33 per head. They were followed by another 50 or so ewes in similar condition. Later, we called the regional producer, and asked what was going on — he grumbled, "Those girls only produced singles... don't want animals like that around!"

Well, somebody went home happy with their new sheep!

If you are a first-time sheep, goat, or other livestock buyer, *please* don't do it at an auction — there are just too many problems that can come with these animals. Buy, instead, from sellers on their farms, where you can see the entire operation and the relatives of the critter being sold. After you've got a couple years' experience under your belt, then you'll be better able to spot problems and avoid them!

Finally, if you haven't been to an auction before, go to one — but, be smart: leave your money at home. Get a feel for the process before you try to wheel-and-deal your way to success.

Better yet, bring an auction-savvy friend along to explain the ropes.

 CB

ଓଃ

Chapter Eight
Protecting Yourself

Country Injuries

If you live in the country, you're going to be injured some time. How, I can't say. But it'll happen. So don't be surprised when it does.

People get body parts caught in farm machinery. They fall out of hay lofts and break something. Big farm animals step on them, or kick them, or smash them into a small space where they wouldn't normally fit. Chain saw injuries are common. So are burns. So are accidental shootings during hunting season. These are some of the basic methods of personal destruction. The local hospital where Anita works as an RN has what staff fondly refers to as *dumb-guy stories*. Those consist of people who find really stupid ways of racking themselves up, such as filling a cistern full of trash, then pouring gasoline all over everything, and lighting it on fire. The good old boys who perpetrated that one caused such an excellent explosion, the emergency room nurses were picking bits of concrete and stuff out of them for hours.

ଓଃ

Nick: I can give you a listing of some of my country-related injuries: a ruptured sciatic disk in my lower back, a cracked eye socket, a ripped muscle in my right shoulder, a broken nose, one broken finger, a cracked windpipe, two snake bites, some dog bites, a broken toe, one concussion, two or three sprained ankles, a cracked rib, a couple dozen bee and wasp stings, countless gashes, cuts, bruises, abrasions, and burns, the list goes on and on.

My best injury — the ruptured disk in my back — came from splitting firewood for three straight hours during a snow storm. My back was already bothering me when I began the job, but I went ahead with it anyway. I'd split a couple pieces, lay down on the cold ground until the pain let up a bit so I could get up again, and then I'd split a few more pieces. And I did this until I'd managed an entire load of wood. It was agony to do it, but we needed the wood. I just paid for it with a ruptured disk in my back, and some pretty decent back and leg pain for the next seven straight weeks. Experiencing this ended up giving me a real high pain threshold. Which has been helpful ever since.

Then, there was the time I got my best black eye ever from a goat I was milking. She collided with my face as she was jumping out of the milk stand. That was definitely a surprise.

Anita has had about three dozen sprained ankles (we've lost track), and Rocky Mountain spotted fever (which isn't an injury, but was still not good).

Who thought living in the country could be so dangerous? If something happens to you, don't take it personally. Just take it in stride. It's part of the game. Like the fella said: that which does not kill us makes us stronger!

Injuries happen. You can be careful and minimize them. But they are part of country life. Just yesterday, trimming our horse's hooves, I got kicked in the stomach twice, which wasn't a very pleasant experience. I had some good bruises this morning. I look on my injuries sort of like hard won medals. An interesting footnote to an active life. Be positive!

On the other hand, it's not a bad idea to have health insurance, you know?

☙

Self-Defense

There is certainly less crime in the country than there is in the city, but that doesn't mean crime doesn't happen in the country, or that it might not happen to you. So, you have to be ready for that possibility, at least psychologically.

Living out in the country, in a way, is like living in the Middle Ages. You are on your own in many respects, especially when it comes to self-defense. You are your own dispenser of law and order in your own little kingdom. That doesn't mean you go around despoiling your neighbors, or executing anyone who comes down your road you don't know. What it does mean is forget 911. The police or sheriff may be too far away from your location to provide you with any kind of effective protection should intruders threaten you, your family, or your property. You are on your own. So, you'd better make up your mind to have a decisive plan of action in case such an event transpires. This may range from having an unassailable safe room in your house (a place to lock yourself away), to having the ability and inclination to stop a burglar, for instance, dead in his tracks.

Of course, if you decide on direct intervention, you have to be mentally prepared to dish out some stopping power. Never confront any adversary you are not one hundred percent ready and willing to put down. Indecision is what gets you killed. If you have a gun or a baseball bat, be ready to administer a palpable consequence on anyone who violates the sanctity of your home, and threatens your well-being. Don't be afraid to hurt this individual. He does not deserve your pity or concern. He is your enemy, and a threat to your well-being.

Also, remember that surprise is one of your best tools. Don't give warning, unless you are fully confident in your own stopping power — say, a pump action shotgun, for instance. Otherwise, hit swiftly and hit hard before a housebreaker knows you are there. And, once he is down, keep him down. Don't run away. Follow up on your advantage. If your visitor gets up, he will be mad, and he will take it out on you. Don't let that happen. A broken collar bone or shattered knee cap will slow down any criminal.

Another point: It is best if you don't put thinking about strategy off to the last minute. A threatening event may never find its way into your life, but, if it does, you should have a plan. You should know, really *know*, what you will do. In a way, this knowledge is a form of life insurance. The worst thing you can do is try to figure out a game plan while a problem is happening. Know your capabilities and your options before hand.

Remember, if you find someone crawling into your house through a kitchen window: 1.) He isn't there to do you any kindness; 2.) You didn't invite him onto your property; 3.) You have a constitutional and moral right to protect yourself; and 4.) A criminal threatening you has absolutely no right to be doing what he is doing. Therefore, hit him hard.

For further reading on the subjects of strategy and defense, we'd recommend anyone concerned about their welfare to read Sun-Tsu's *The Art of War*, Miyamto Musashi's *The Book of Five Rings*, Thomas Cleary's *The Japanese Art of War*, and

Nick's volume, *Fighting with Sticks* (Loompanics Unlimited, 1998).

In the end, your life, ultimately, is your own responsibility. So, take it in hand, and know in your heart of hearts what you would do if menaced. Be ready to mold your situation in such a way that you have a say in interactions with dangerous individuals.

The country, for all its seemingly pastoral nature, is not a pacifist's world. Don't be a victim.

Guns

We don't know how you feel about guns right now; but, we can tell you, most people we've known who've moved to the country — no matter how much they disliked guns initially — ended up buying some kind of firearm. For hunting purposes, and/or for protection. When you live out on a dirt road, having a rifle, or whatever, is as much a form of insurance as a life-insurance policy is. You'll realize the need. Even if you never use your gun, it brings a certain peace of mind the numbers 911 never give you.

You should know how to use your firearm, of course. If you don't know how to use it, you're as much a danger to yourself and your family as a burglar would be. But you can take courses that will teach you everything you'll need to know about your gun and gun safety. This is as reasonable as taking a driver's education class when you buy a car.

Responsibility is the key word here. Some people do stupid and awful things with guns, but some people misuse a lot of items in the world. Most people don't. The gun issue cannot be solved by emotionalism — only by intelligence and the strict enforcement of laws.

Whatever you think of guns while you are living in the crowded suburb of some crowded city, you'll rethink your position the first time you hear some unexplained noises outside your farm house on a dark fall night, maybe around midnight, so you know it's not the mailman. Or. What do you think you'd do if some afternoon you saw a stranger messing around your barn or tool shed? Would you go outside with tea and cookies, and welcome him into your home? Maybe this individual had a troubled childhood, and is only looking for someone to be nice to him. Then again, maybe he'd just want to smash you flat if he had a chance because he doesn't want to go back to prison, which he just got out of last week. You are on your own in a situation like this. The sheriff is probably an hour away. It's your call.

Think about this issue logically.

You'll want a gun sometime.

You will.

You won't stay long in the country if you are continually scared out of your wits.

03

ങ

Chapter Nine
Still Going? Some Things to Think About

Loneliness

There is something to be said for the solitude of living in the country. It can be a grand and calming thing. There is much majesty in Nature. But it does take some getting used to. Especially if you've lived your life amid the noise and bustle of the city. Even if you hate the noise and bustle of the city. Some people end up loving the seclusion of the countryside. Some people go absolutely nuts. The husband and wife who owned our farm immediately before we did ended up with the wife becoming an alcoholic because she was from St. Louis, and she hated being alone. In one direction, the nearest neighbor is a quarter mile away; in the other direction, it's a full mile. The nearest town was, and still is, 16 miles away. After a year and a half, she finally fled back to the city; her husband followed soon after that.

ങ

Nick: Night in the country can be very dark and spooky, even if you have a yard light. It doesn't get any lighter, though, no matter how long you live in the country. You just have to get used to it. I used to think our particular setting was perfect for a zombie attack, with woods right out beyond our milking barn. I creeped myself out all the time, thinking about that, when I was out milking our goats at night. Zombies stumbling and shuffling out of the woods. It's easy to think like that when you're alone, and it's really, really dark all around you, and, of course, if you've seen one or two zombie movies.

Anita: Living alone out in the country made me think about drive-by shootings. There weren't any police around for miles and miles, Nick had to remind me that there also were no gangs around for miles and miles. If we wanted drive-by shootings, we'd have to bus in gangs from out of the area.

☙

The imagination can run rampant without the steadying influences of the packed urban setting. We got better. Some people don't. We can recall reading an article a few years ago in the *Wall Street Journal* about people who had to go into therapy after spending weekends at homes in the country. They were traumatized with thoughts of ax murderers, and other hoodlums, climbing on their roofs at night (which turned out to be squirrels). And one woman was frightened by a bright light that kept shining in through her bedroom window (this proved to be the moon). In a way, these reactions are no worse than attacking zombies; we just missed out on the therapy part of the deal.

There is also the winter cut-off-from-civilization factor. When it snows, for instance, or the ground ices up, and you can't drive out. This is sometimes called cabin fever. And you can literally go bonkers. When we're iced in for a month, even a discussion about what to have for dinner could turn into a major fight. The writer Tim Cahill, in his book *Jaguars Ripped My Flesh*, told a story of a husband and wife who once owned his cabin, and why there was a shotgun blast in his bathroom door: To illustrate the connection between cabin fever and long Montana winters. This is something to think about, especially if you've long considered yourself a party animal.

There's no denying it, there are fewer people in the country than in the city. If there were just as many people in the country, it would be a city, too.

The country can get real lonely.

Hope you like it.

Bugs

No one fresh from the city is ever ready for the vast and varied forms of bug life that reside in the rural setting. You may know about cockroaches, but the country has so much more to offer: bugs of all sizes, shapes, colors, and temperaments. More bugs than you ever knew existed. Most bugs, of course, want nothing to do with you personally. But you'll probably, at one time or another, make the acquaintance of something better left under a rock.

Mantises, walking sticks, lady bugs, honey bees, and most beetles are just fine. They will live and let live.

Generally speaking, you'll find plenty of everyday, average bad bugs in the country. There'll always be plenty of flies. Spraying helps some. But flies are the weeds of the bug world. And you'll never run out of regular ants. Or roaches, the big, black water-bug type.

In the bugs with an attitude department, you'll find a heck of a lot of little menaces. Wasps are a problem. They'll live in your house walls, and your attic. They'll live in your barn.

And they'll sting you for fun. One summer, our son Justin was stung on twenty-five separate occasions. We were glad when that summer was over. Carpenter ants do the same sort of damage that termites will do to wood, so watch the firewood you store near your house (that's where they hide). Fire ants are a potential life-threatening problem, as they can kill people, at least, it feels that way.

In the average bad bug category, we can find a number of unpleasant members. Mosquitoes will be with you in the summer. Count on it. Then, there are ticks, those little, blood-sucking menaces, and their hungry chigger cousins, all of whom who wish to put you one notch down on the food chain. Lots of itching and scratching goes along with them. One of the most awful things you can experience is to look down and see hundreds of newly hatched baby ticks — no bigger than grains of salt — swarming up your pants legs looking for their first meal. Makes you kind of want to stay out of your fields.

Next, come the numerous garden infesting bugs: Japanese beetles, squash bugs, bunches of leaf and fruit eating caterpillars, buffalo leaf hoppers, aphids, and a bunch you've never seen before, and can't find in your bug identification books.

Then, come various poisonous, but not all that aggressive, bugs: brown recluse spiders, black widow spiders, blister beetles, scorpions, and assassin bugs. These are your basic keep-out-of-my-face bugs. Anita was once bitten by a brown recluse spider, the bite of which is necrotic, which means the bite spot rots, hurts, can get badly infected, and leaves a nasty scar.

Anyone not meeting up with bugs in the country is probably sitting in a vat of insecticide.

Weather

Because our roots were in Los Angeles, we didn't know weather or seasons. In L.A., there's summer and not-quite-summer, and everyone digs out their overcoats if it drops below 70 degrees. Missouri was a shock for us.

For some reason, weather changes are more abrupt and severe in the country than in the city. Don't ask me why. It simply is. That's why everyone in the country talks about the weather as part of their daily jawing.

The lightning is more menacing, the rain comes down harder and quicker, and the winds are stronger in the country. You really have to be in tune with what's happening. Everything in the rural setting is dependent on the weather.

Especially if you work outside. Putting up a barbed wire fence today? Not if there's an electrical storm. Planting a garden? Not if it's supposed to snow tomorrow. Ignore the weather, and you can really get burned.

We heard a saying right after we moved to our farm that the weather changes so fast in rural Missouri, if you don't like what's happening, wait fifteen minutes and you'll get what you want. We've heard that joke since then, though, in reference to about fifteen other states. We suppose it's the same for all country weather.

Remember, you may have experienced bad weather in the city, but in the city there are agencies to call on for help when nature gives you a black eye. In the country, living on a dirt road, you are on your own.

Personal Habits

It's important, when you move to the country, to maintain a sense of civilization and personal habits. Away from the stabilizing effects of the city, away from other people, it's easy to let yourself go, and not even think about it.

It really can get to you.

Let's look at a worst-case scenario situation. You're just not out in the country, it's also snowing, and you feel psychologically cut off from the world. Completely. You decide, "Hey, I've got enough food to last me for a month, I'm not even going to try to get to town in this weather. I'm just going to hunker down. I don't have to shave or wash. Forget manners. Forget about the world."

What happens?

One day, maybe two weeks later, you suddenly look in the mirror, and there's this unknown, unkempt, sunken-eyed cave slob staring back at you. "Whoa! Who's the pig? And how'd he get into my clothes?" And, speaking of clothes, how long have you been wearing them? When was the last time you changed your underwear?

Good questions, but you know what? You don't have any answers for them. That's the really sad, and scary, part.

ॐ

Nick: I think my all-time-too-long-alone behavior was when I used to wear a single pair of socks for weeks on end. Then, when I couldn't wear them any longer, I'd just open the wood cook stove, throw them in, and burn them up. This didn't bother me either. This was not a good time in my life.

ॐ

This kind of stuff is not good for your brain. We know. You can't cut yourself off from the world or human behavior. When you relinquish stabilizing influences, useful, positive thoughts can just melt away. You won't necessarily turn into a full-fledged loony, but you just might be beyond making decisions that will keep your farm running smoothly.

Then, where are you?

Your Own Worst Enemy

Nick: I personally believed that once we got to our farm that suddenly our lives would be transformed into some kind of wonderful, creative experience, a shining utopia without pain or care. Just because we moved. Unfortunately, I didn't leave myself or my problems behind when I climbed into that moving van that transported us and our possessions across the country. All the limited thinking and personal problems that were sabotaging me in Los Angeles came along for the ride.

When it dawned on me that a life only changes when you change yourself, not your location, I started working on me! Then, I made some real progress shaping that better life plan.

og

A tendency towards outright laziness, or disorganization, or procrastination, or fanaticizing won't get any better in the country. Your weaker personal features may actually become more pronounced, because now you'll have a hundred things to do that'll be right in your face constantly.

The seasons themselves will underscore your less desirable qualities. Things have to be done when it's time. You can't plant your early spring garden, for instance, in the middle of summer. It doesn't work. Plants need a specific time to grow. You can't fake-out or double talk Mother Nature.

Also, if you think your change of location will make you more creative, smarter, or develop a more pleasing personality, think again. If you're a stupid, shallow creep in the city, you'll still be a stupid, shallow creep in the country. You'll just be a stupid, shallow creep with farm animals. If those traits that make you less than desirable are going to be altered for the better, you have to supplant something better.

You have to be careful, when you make that big move, that you don't become your own worst enemy.

Paranoia

Nick: It probably took a whole year of living in the country before Anita and I finally realized just how paranoid we'd been when we lived in the city. One day, it just hit us. We hadn't realized we were paranoid in Los Angeles. But we sure must have been. Otherwise, where did the paranoia come from?

Anyway, our metabolism slowed down, or something, and we saw how we were reacting in a generally distrustful way to events and people that weren't even close to warranting such behavior.

For instance, a few days after we'd moved in to our farm, I took my kids down to a nearby river. Lazy water, shade, quiet. Very country, very restful. What could be wrong with that? Two young guys came walking up the road with rifles. Suddenly, the old paranoia alarm clicked into action. Images from Deliverance came flooding into my brain. Hey, boy, can you squeal like a pig? The two guys, who were maybe 18 or 19, waved, and walked on by. Obviously a ploy to lull me into a false sense of security. If I fell for it, I was bacon. Just like Pearl Harbor.

I pretended like I didn't see them, and herded my kids home as fast as I could. Well, you know you observe gun-toting individuals out for a stroll in the city, and you run and hide in a hedge. That's normal.

Of course, nothing happened with the two guys. Actually, they lived just down the road from us with their parents. They'd been out doing some target practice. Talk about ominous! Yow!

It's always best to be safe. But you have to lose some of that city paranoia. It is not appropriate to adapting to the country.

Paranoia can eat you up.

☯

Pretensions

Want to drive off your neighbors and fit in to the country like a cold sore at a kissing party? Act like a big-city-know-it-all with everyone you meet.

My wife and I thought we knew absolutely everything about the country. We'd read *Mother Earth News*, after all. What else was there to know? The first time we met our closest neighbors from down the road, we did our damnedest to impress them with our country wonderfulness. We talked about French intensive gardening and organics like we'd invented the subjects. Pretentious? No, we were worse than that. Our neighbors had lived in the country their entire lives. What could they possibly know about it? They doubtlessly thought we were the largest jerk-types they'd ever met. Luckily, they were tolerant of ninnies. Luckily, also, we wised up.

Give up your pretensions the day you arrive at your new home in the country. Don't alienate people who might one day help you survive your country ignorance.

This is important. It may not seem like it now, when you know everything. But there'll come a day when you no longer know everything. And this advice will mean something to you.

Letting Go of the Past

If you find yourself hanging onto the past in the form of never-ending gripes about how bad the city you left was, get off the subject now. No one wants to know. Not really. And it'll be healthier for you to forget it. Such ruminating takes your focus away from your present life. Also, you don't want to be known for the boredom you generate.

Anita and I were stuck on the subject of how awful Los Angeles and city life was for about a year. Everyone we met got the same old, killer litany. Yackity, yackity, yackity. We just wouldn't shut up. We'd go on and on and on about city crime, city pollution, city over-crowding, city rules and regulations, city schools, city living costs, and city crazies until the people we'd be talking to would just kind of slump over, their eyes rolling up in their head. Talk about broken records. We're not sure if we were trying to convince everyone else or ourselves as to how bad our lives had been.

We are glad we got tired of bad-mouthing city life. We were beginning to even bore ourselves. If you realize you're doing the same thing, let the city go before someone shoots you to put you out of their misery. City nonsense is not interesting for more than a minute. You can't make a career out of it.

Head towards the future.

Missing the City

There will be times when you will miss the city. This is understandable. If you grew up in an urban environment, that is what you know. It's ingrained into your very being. Even if you left hating everything connected with cities, you will mellow with time, and you will think fondly of your past life.

This nostalgic lapse can be a dangerous time, as it is in these moments, where reasons and motives blur, that you can decide to chuck your present situation, with its headaches and pressures, and head back where things are ordered and predictable, and there are sidewalks.

This is a time when you have to forcibly remind yourself of why you moved to the country in the first place. If you can't think of any reasons why you are still living on a farm, maybe you are making a mistake holding onto what you are doing. It shouldn't be that difficult to find reasons for living in the country. This doesn't mean you have to really puff yourself up into an insane rage against city life either. We can think of lots of stuff we like about Southern California: old book stores, Japanese restaurants, beaches, the theatre, old friends, the creative energy of the big city, variety. Just the same, we couldn't ever live there again for any length of time. We'd go nuts.

When missing the city comes up, you should have some good answers to plop into those blank spots in your brain, reminding you that life in the country, no matter what, is where your future lies. Know yourself. This awareness may save you from a rash life decision about your place of residence that some time later you could really, really regret.

Automotive Stress

If you have an older automobile when you move to the country, be warned: The dirt roads will eat it up like so much cardboard. Be ready to change lots of tires, and learn, at the very least, basic car repair.

Coming to the Ozark Mountains fresh from Los Angeles, we began our rural life driving the archtypical Southern California vehicle, a Volkswagen van. Even though it was in good repair, thanks to the hazards of country roads, it lasted for less than a year before it was shot. (We ended up trading it for 100 gallons of raw cow milk to someone who thought he could tinker it back to life.)

We would recommend to anyone who is thinking of living in the country to buy a second vehicle, preferably something old and easy to fix, as a backup.

Since then, we've had a 1967 Chevy Suburban (a good, old solid vehicle, with the staying power of the Arnold Schwarzenegger robot in *Terminator II),* a Nissan Sentra (easy on the gas), a Chevy Malibu Classic station wagon (we needed something to haul hay and livestock in after the Suburban bellied up), and a Chevy conversion van (a concession to a more mobile lifestyle).

CB

Nick: Lots of cars, with lots of problems. The back roads really do get to them, wear them down, almost shake them apart. I can tell you, car repair was not something I actively sought out. I just had to do it. I read books, and tinkered when this car or that stopped moving forward. In the time we've been in the country, I've seen the gamut of car problems, from electrical to mechanical to structural. Some things I just couldn't repair, of course. I either didn't have the expertise or the right tools. But so many things with our autos have turned out to be problems I could both diagnose and cure. You don't know until you try. But, certainly, if you aren't willing to get greasy dirty, forget it.

CB

We would recommend to anyone who is thinking of living in the country to buy a second vehicle, preferably a truck, an old, easy-fix truck, as a backup. You'll need it. Not maybe, but for sure.

You can't live in the country without a car. A working car, that is.

The Full Moon

The full moon can be either a friend or an enemy to you when you move to the country. Therefore, realizing that there really is an influence becomes the first step in gaining some control over the situation. While so much around the moon remains folklore-oriented, there is no doubt among those who live intimately with its effects that it really does cast a power over the world.

When all is said and done, you either believe, or you don't. Of course, mainstream thought still scoffs at the idea of lunar intervention in the affairs of man. The police, hospital emergency wards, and mental institutions will tell you a different story. The English language has a word for a person adversely affected by the full moon: lunatic.

On the plus side, old-time farmers were of the mind that the full moon played an important part in their lives.

It was a good time for planting crops and breeding livestock, they said. This was simply understood. You wanted to do things right, you paid attention to the phases of the moon. *The Farmer's Almanac* still makes special note of the full moon's cycle. Modern scientists say that this is not true. The moon may affect the tides, but anything else is mumbo jumbo folk lore. Modern scientists say a lot of things.

But let's get back to that adverse side to the full moon, we spoke of earlier. The goofy stuff. Tempers may flair more easily. Violence erupts with little or no provocation. People become klutzy, and do themselves injuries. People who are already mentally stressed become impossible to deal with. Imagine moving to the country, you're on edge from the change in your life, and you get a full moon on top of everything else. Maybe it's enough to throw you and the spouse into a real furniture breaker. Just because you weren't on guard against the full moon, and, when it hit, there was no one to step back and say, "What the heck are we doing? Oops, full moon!" Being able to monitor outside influences can help derail arguments.

During the run of the full moon, we know for a fact that the behavior of our animals changes, usually becoming more aggressive. Sometimes it's subtle, such as a little extra head bashing among the sheep and goats, or rabbits getting a bit jumpy in their cages, or dogs barking more mindlessly than usual when there's nothing to bark at. Maybe you wouldn't notice if you weren't paying close attention. Sometimes it is more overt, like a horse trying to kick your head off simply because you exist, or an otherwise friendly ram knocking you head over heels when just the day before he was eating grain out of your hand.

Another thing: Before we built good, strong barbed-wire fences surrounding our property, our sheep and goats would develop a wanderlust every time the full moon came around. Every time. It didn't matter how lush our fields were, or even if we put hay down in front of them to distract them, they wanted to be elsewhere, and they usually managed it with irritating facility.

If all this sounds as though we're casting a vote for the full moon influencing our lives, that's okay, because we are. We think it's very important to cover all your bases when you move to the country, identifying all kinds of outside forces, seen and unseen, that can be either harmful or helpful to your cause. This can only add ammunition to your survivability quotient.

You have time and distance to observe and digest things in the country, things you might never come too close to noticing in the city. When you do, don't deny the obvious.

Even something as seemingly innocuous as the moon can do you in, if you're not careful.

Procrastination

Procrastination can be anyone's downfall. It is the theme of Shakespeare's *Hamlet*. To be, or not to be! Remember? And almost everybody died in that play. City folks procrastinate.

Suburban folks procrastinate. Country folks procrastinate. Apparently, not acting in time is part of human nature. Unfortunately.

But what about specifically procrastinating in the country? What's the big deal here about putting something off until some unspecified later date that you wouldn't necessarily run into elsewhere? Well, how's this? Nature. Nature won't be put off. Nature does not wait for you to get around to doing what must be done. Nature has its own schedule. An animal that needs to be wormed, and isn't, dies. A crop that needs to be planted by a particular date, because it has a specific maturing time, and isn't, will not have time to grow. Crops that need to be picked because they are ripe, and aren't, will rot. A cow or goat that needs to be milked now, and isn't, will develop mastitis.

Every *isn't*, *don't*, *didn't*, *wasn't*, and *won't* sets you back, slows you down, distracts you, sidetracks you, and gives you more to do with less time to do it in. Everything undone today becomes a burden, putting unneeded pressure on you, and, in one way or another, contributes to an air of potential failure.

You can justify, rationalize, argue, and cast blame elsewhere, but these neither get the job done, nor keep the bill collector away. You have a window of opportunity that is impervious to wishes or regrets.

Planning in advance may help you. Making detailed schedules may help you. Remembering why you are doing what you are doing may help you. Honesty may help you. But don't get caught up in the preliminaries. In the end, these are only a means to an end. Only doing now accomplishes.

How many *forgot tos*, *tried tos*, *meant tos*, *didn't have time tos*, and *I'll get to that laters* can a life take before it collapses under its own bloated weight?

Do what you need to do now! Make a daily/weekly/monthly list of tasks, and check them off as they are completed.

Timing, to be sure, is everything.

ℭℨ

ଔ

Appendix

Selected Reading

Books

Encyclopedia of Country Living, by Carla Emery. Published by Sasquatch Books, 1994.

Guide to Survival Communications, by Dave Ingram. Published by Universal Electronics, Inc. 4555 Groves Rd, Suite 12, Columbus, OH 43232-4135 ($20 + $4 shipping and handling).

How to Develop a Low-Cost Family Food Storage System, by Anita Evangelista. Published by Breakout Productions, 1995.

How to Live Without Electricity — And Like It, by Anita Evangelista. Published by Breakout Productions, 1997.

Making The Best of Basics, by James Talmadge Stevens. Published by Gold Leaf Press, 1997.

Practical Skills: A Revival of Forgotten Crafts, Techniques and Traditions, by Gene Logsdon. Published by Rodale Press, Emmaus, PA, 1985.

Putting Food By, by Ruth Hertzberg, Beatrice Vaughan and Janet Greene. Published by the Stephen Greene Press, Brattleboro, VT 05301, 1974 — many subsequent editions.

Stocking Up, How to Preserve the Foods You Grow Naturally, edited by Carol Hupping Stoner. Published by Rodale Press — many editions.

Magazines
Backwoods Home Magazine
1257 Siskiyou Blvd, #213
Ashland, OR 97520

Small Farmer's Journal
PO Box 1627
Sisters, OR 97402

Countryside and Small Stock Journal
W11564 Hwy 64
Withee, WI 54498

Water Resources

Deep Rock
8154 Anderson Rd
Opelika, AL 36801-9700
1-800-333-7762
http://www.deeprock.com

Kansas Wind Power
13569 214th Rd
Holton, KS 66436
1-785-364-4407

Lehman's Hardware and Appliances
One Lehman Circle
PO Box 41
Kidron, OH 44636
1-330-857-5757
http://www.lehmans.com

Real Goods
555 Leslie St
Ukiah, CA 95482-5576
http://www.realgoods.com

Cʒ

☐ **14181 EAT WELL FOR 99¢ A MEAL,** *by Bill and Ruth Kaysing.* Want more energy, more robust, vigorous health? Then you must eat food that can impart these well-being characteristics and this book will be your faithful guide. As an important bonus, you will learn how to save lots of money and learn how to enjoy three homemade meals a day for a cost of less than one dollar per meal. The book will show you how to shop, how to stock your pantry, where to pick fresh foods for free, how to cook your 99¢ meal, what foods you can grow yourself, how to preserve your perishables, several recipes to get you started, and much, much more. *1996, 5½ x 8½, 204 pp, illustrated, indexed, soft cover.* $14.95

☐ **14183 THE 99¢ A MEAL COOKBOOK,** *by Ruth and Bill Kaysing.* Ruth and Bill Kaysing have compiled these recipes with one basic thought in mind: People don't like over-processed foods and they can save a lot of money by taking things into their own hands. These are practical recipes because they advise the cook where to find the necessary ingredients at low cost. And every bit as important — the food that you make will taste delicious! This is a companion volume to the *Eat Well for 99¢ A Meal. 1996, 5½ x 8½, 272 pp, indexed, soft cover.* $14.95

☐ **14178 THE WILD AND FREE COOKBOOK, With a Special Roadkill Section,** *by Tom Squier.* Why pay top dollar for grocery-store food, when you can dine at no cost by foraging and hunting? Wild game, free of the steroids and additives found in commercial meat, is better for you, and many weeds and wild plants are more nutritious than the domestic fruits and vegetables found in the supermarket. Authored by a former Special Forces survival school instructor, this cookbook is chock full of easy-to-read recipes that will enable you to turn wild and free food (including roadkill!) into gourmet meals. *1996, 7¼ x 11½, 306 pp, illustrated, indexed, soft cover.* $19.95

CB

☐ **19206 FIGHTING WITH STICKS,** *by Nick Evangelista.* Errol Flynn, Bruce Lee and Sean Connery did it. So did Medieval swordsmen and African warriors who wielded their oars as weapons. It's an ancient art of stick fighting, revered and explained by author Nick Evangelista. Detailed instructions guide the reader through proper attire, equipment, and sportsmanship codes for stick fighting, as a game or in self-defense. Why sticks? Because they're handy, easy to operate, and don't require ammunition or a license. In the event of a societal breakdown or nuclear holocaust, you'd still be able to find a stick and use it. *1998, 5½ x 8½, 158 pp, illustrated, soft cover.* $15.00

☐ **14175 SELF-SUFFICIENCY GARDENING, Financial, Physical and Emotional Security From Your Own Backyard,** *by Martin P. Waterman.* A practical guide to organic gardening techniques that will enable anyone to grow vegetables, fruits, nuts, herbs, medicines and other useful products, thereby increasing self-sufficiency and enhancing the quality of life. Includes sections on edible landscaping; greenhouses; hydroponics and computer gardening (including the Internet); seed saving and propagation; preserving and storing crops; and much more, including fact-filled appendices. The author is a highly regarded journalist and gardener, world-recognized fruit breeder and is a director of the North American Fruit Explorers. *1995, 8½ x 11, 128 pp, illustrated, indexed, soft cover.* $13.95

☐ **14177 COMMUNITY TECHNOLOGY,** *by Karl Hess, with an Introduction by Carol Moore.* In the 1970s, the late Karl Hess participated in a five-year social experiment in Washington D.C.'s Adams-Morgan neighborhood. Hess and several thousand others labored to make their neighborhood as self-sufficient as possible, turning to such innovative techniques as raising fish in basements, growing crops on rooftops and in vacant lots, installing self-contained bacteriolocial toilets, and planning a methanol plant to convert garbage to fuel. There was a newsletter and weekly community meetings, giving Hess and others a taste of participatory government that changed their lives forever. *1979, 5½ x 8½, 120 pp, soft cover.* $9.95

CB

☐ **17054 HOW TO BUY LAND CHEAP, Fifth Edition,** *by Edward Preston.* This is the bible of bargain-basement land buying. The author bought eight lots for a total sum of $25. He shows you how to buy good land all over the country for not much more. This book has been revised, with updated addresses and new addresses added. This book will take you through the process for finding cheap land, evaluating and bidding on it, and closing the deal. Sample form letters are also included to help you get started and get results. You can buy land for less than the cost of a night out — this book shows how. *1996, 5½ x 8½, 136 pp, illustrated, soft cover.* $14.95

☐ **17040 SHELTERS, SHACKS AND SHANTIES,** *by D.C. Beard.* A fascinating book with more than 300 pen and ink illustrations and step-by-step instructions for building various types of shelters. The emphasis is on simplicity with easy-to-use tools such as hatchets and axes. Fallen tree shelters • Indian wicki-ups • sod houses • elevated shacks and shanties • tree houses • caches • railroad tie shacks • pole houses • log cabins • and many more. One of the great classics of outdoor lore. *1914, 5 x 7, 259 pp, illustrated, soft cover.* $14.95

☐ **14205 TRAVEL-TRAILER HOMESTEADING UNDER $5,000, Revised and Expanded, 2nd Edition,** *by Brian Kelling.* Tired of paying rent? Need privacy away from nosy neighbors? This updated book will show how a modest financial investment can enable you to place a travel-trailer or other RV on a suitable piece of land and make the necessary improvements for a comfortable home in which to live! This book covers the cost break-down, tools needed, how to select the land and travel-trailer or RV, and how to install a septic system, as well as water, power (including solar panels), heat and refrigeration systems. This new edition covers how to cheaply install and run a hot tub, and reasons why you'll never want to leave your independence. *1999, 5½ x 8½, 112 pp, photographs, diagrams, illustrations, soft cover.* $10.00

‫ℭჟ‬

Please send me the following titles:

- ☐ 14193, Backyard Meat Production, $14.95
- ☐ 14176, How to Develop a Low-Cost Family-Food Storage System, $10.00
- ☐ 14187, How to Live Without Electricity — and Like it!, $13.95
- ☐ 14181, Eat Well for 99¢ a Meal, $14.95
- ☐ 14183, The 99¢ a Meal Cookbook, $14.95
- ☐ 14178, The Wild & Free Cookbook, $19.95
- ☐ 19206, Fighting With Sticks, $15.00
- ☐ 14175, Self-Sufficiency Gardening, $13.95
- ☐ 14177, Community Technology, $9.95
- ☐ 17054, How to Buy Land Cheap, $14.95
- ☐ 17040, Shelters, Shacks, and Shanties, $14.95
- ☐ 14205, Travel-Trailer Homesteading Under $5,000, $10.00

NEA99

LOOMPANICS UNLIMITED
PO BOX 1197
PORT TOWNSEND, WA 98368

Please send me the books I have checked above. I am enclosing $ _____ which includes $4.95 for shipping and handling of orders up to $25.00. Add $1.00 for each additional $25.00 ordered *Washington residents please include 7.9% for sales tax.*

NAME _____

_____

ADDRESS _____

_____

CITY/STATE/ZIP _____

We accept Visa, Discover and MasterCard. To place a credit card order *only,* call 1-800-380-2230, 24 hours a day, 7 days a week.
Check us out on the web: www.loompanics.com